# ME FUNNY

. . . . . . . . . . . . .

# ME

COMPILED *and* EDITED *by*

# *Drew* HAYDEN TAYLOR

· · · · · · · · · · · · · · · · · · · · · · · · · · · · · ·

# FUNNY

· · · · · · · · · · · · · · · · · · · · · · · · · · · · · ·

A *far-reaching* exploration of the **HUMOUR**, wittiness and repartee
**DOMINANT** among the *First Nations people* of North America,
as witnessed, *experienced* and **CREATED DIRECTLY** by themselves,
and with the **INCLUSION** of outside *but reputable* sources
necessarily *familiar* with the **INDIGENOUS** sense of humour as
**SEEN** from an *objective perspective*

DOUGLAS & McINTYRE
*Vancouver/Toronto/Berkeley*

05  06  07  08  09    5  4  3  2  1

Douglas & McIntyre Ltd.
2323 Quebec Street, Suite 201
Vancouver, British Columbia
Canada V5T 4S7
www.douglas-mcintyre.com

*Library and Archives Canada Cataloguing in Publication*
Me funny / edited by Drew Hayden Taylor.

ISBN-10: 1-55365-137-5 · ISBN-13: 978-1-55365-137-6

1. Indian wit and humor—Canada. 2. Indians of North America—
Canada—Humor. 3. Canadian literature (English)—
Indian authors—History and criticism. 4. Canadian literature—
20th century—History and criticism. I. Taylor, Drew Hayden, 1962–
E78.C2M45 2006    c817'.5409897    c2005-905650-9

Library of Congress information is available upon request

Editing by Barbara Pulling and Pam Robertson
Cover and interior design by Peter Cocking
Cover image © Swim Ink/CORBIS
Printed and bound in Canada by Friesens
Printed on acid-free paper that is forest friendly (100% post-consumer
recycled paper) and has been processed chlorine free.
Distributed in the U.S. by Publishers Group West

We gratefully acknowledge the financial support of the Canada
Council for the Arts, the British Columbia Arts Council,
and the Government of Canada through the Book Publishing Industry
Development Program (BPDIP) for our publishing activities.

# CONTENTS

· · · · · · · · · · · · ·

# INTRODUCTION

. . . . . . . . . . . . . . . . . . . .

*N*OT LONG ago a good friend of mine made a comment about a project I was working on. I was attempting to interest the National Film Board of Canada in a documentary I wanted to do on Native erotica, to which my white friend replied, somewhat disdainfully, "Why? You guys do 'it' just the same way we do."

"Except our tan lines are a little less obvious," I responded.

Some people have wondered the same thing about Native humour. Is it fundamentally that different from Jewish humour, African-Canadian humour, Lithuanian humour, Icelandic humour and so on? As somebody on the inside looking out, I can safely say yes. But not exceedingly. We're talking nuances, subtleties. It's as if chicken is the joke, but the sauce or the unique flavours of the joke's humour come from various cultures. You've got tandoori chicken vs. chicken cacciatore vs. a McChicken, if you get my meaning. Generally, what makes you laugh will make us laugh. We're not exactly from another planet, though I can't vouch for all Aboriginal people. I base this observation on twenty years as a professional writer and forty-two years as an Ojibway—or, since I'm a halfbreed, technically maybe that should be twenty-one years as an Ojibway and twenty-one years as a white person.

In putting this book together, I approached noted Anishinabe storyteller and author Basil Johnston with an invitation to participate. He declined, stating, "I don't know what useful purpose an analysis of 'Indian humour' would serve. I'm afraid that any analysis would just leave mistaken impressions in the academic world; too much of Indian humour rests in the language." Basil has always advocated the importance of indigenous languages, so his comment comes as no surprise. As for his hypothesis: maybe, maybe not. I do acknowledge that a different level of humour can be appreciated in the applicable indigenous tongue. Tomson Highway deals with that topic admirably well in his essay in this book. But like the air in a worn out tire, the humour can and does leak out in many different places.

If you want to complicate the issue further, try looking at Native humour from a nuclear subatomic perspective (yes, there is a correlation). In one of our discussions on the subject, Thomson King and I considered the possibility that Heisenberg's uncertainty principle might apply here. It was Heisenberg's belief that the art of observing alters the reality being observed. Maybe putting Native humour under the microscope changes its effects or its impact. I don't know. I was always weak in physics.

Several years back, I wrote and directed a documentary for the National Film Board on Native humour. The film is called *Redskins, Tricksters and Puppy Stew*. It was great fun to do, and it provided me with the unique opportunity of being paid to hang out with all my friends and talk funny. And talk about being funny. And talk about what *is* funny—from an Aboriginal perspective, of course. That's where I got the inspiration for this collection.

Humour requires intelligence. It calls for the ability to take in information, deconstruct it and reconstruct it in a new, improved, refined format. The humorist then reintroduces that information to the world to achieve a completely different reaction. Humour also requires surprise. Generally speaking, if the punchline is something you're expecting, then it won't be funny. Of course there are exceptions to every rule. In comedy, repeating something three times (but not successively) is a time-honoured way to structure a joke, with each successive repetition getting a bigger laugh. And there is seldom anything new or surprising in sitcoms. In fact, it's their familiarity that audiences often find comfortable and amusing. Comedy, like many other things in life, can be contradictory. It seems the Creator has seen fit to place us in an unpredictable world. But here I go again, pretending I know what I'm talking about.

In *Me Funny* you will find many different ideas about the nature of Native humour. You may agree with some of them. You may disagree instead. I don't care—you've already bought the book. Let's just say I hope that when you have finished reading it you will be scratching your head from thinking a lot and holding your belly from laughing a lot. That's a good mixture where I come from.

Oh, by the way, what did the Indian say when he walked into a bar?

"Ouch!"

DREW HAYDEN TAYLOR

# ONE BIG INDIAN

. . . . . . . . . . . . . . . . .

{ ALLAN J. RYAN }

*T*HIS IS a story of one big Indian. More specifically, it is the story of an *image* of one big Indian, which found expression in a pencil drawing on paper, an acrylic painting on canvas, a duplicate painting on plywood, a commemorative colour poster and a black-and-white photograph of the painting, which was used to promote an exhibition of Indian art. The photo was reproduced on the invitation to the opening of the art exhibition, as well as on the cover of the show's catalogue. In the summer of 1985, if you lived anywhere near the Six Nations Reserve or the neighbouring city of Brantford, Ontario, you would have undoubtedly encountered this big Indian. Like it or not.

The story begins the previous year, in the summer of 1984, when Mohawk artist Bill Powless took a break from his job, as graphic designer and exhibition preparator at the Woodland Cultural Centre in Brantford, to join fellow artists Leland

Bell and Carl Beam in creating murals for the Spirit of Sharing Native arts festival, held on Manitoulin Island in northern Ontario. Manitoulin Island, located in Georgian Bay just off the north shore of Lake Huron, has long been a centre of Aboriginal artistic activity. It is home to the Ojibwe Cultural Foundation and the De-ba-jeh-mu-jig Theatre Group, as well as an annual powwow hosted by the Wikwemikong Ojibway First Nation. The island, also popular with tourists and summer vacationers, is renowned for its clean air, clear water and endless shoreline.

It was during his summer sojourn on Manitoulin that Powless chanced to see a rather heavyset Aboriginal bather emerge from the water one afternoon, sit down on the tailgate of a pickup truck and snap open a can of beer. What caught the artist's attention, and caused him to smile, was the big man's unusual head covering: a miniature umbrella that seemed to hover just above his head, with no visible means of support, and, in the absence of sunglasses, shade his eyes from the sun's hot glare. He was a comical sight. When Powless returned to Brantford, he made a quick pencil sketch of the man from memory (see fig. 1). The small sketch would serve as a visual reference for a larger acrylic painting he envisioned.

In the drawing, the individual is seated in a classic, three-quarter-length portrait pose, facing left, with his left hand firmly planted on his left thigh and his right forearm resting on his right thigh. There is a casual confidence to his posture, an almost regal bearing. With minimal shading and the barest of outlines, Powless captures the soft and generous contours of the man's rotund and Buddha-like physique. His curious umbrella headpiece looks wonderfully absurd, even more so now that a small feather has been tethered to its peak to underscore the wearer's indigenous identity. Strangely translucent, the umbrella casts a soft shadow across the man's eyes, which seem closed in

*fig. 1:* Keeping Cool, *Bill Powless, graphite on paper, 21.5 × 28 cm, no date.*

sleep or deep reflection. A narrow headband secures the long hair falling over his shoulders and down his back. A single pendant disc, the size of a quarter, dangles from his right ear.

For no reason that Powless can now recall, the artist replaced the can of beer in the figure's right hand with a Popsicle—a double Popsicle, to be exact. As a symbol of summer refreshment, a Popsicle is, perhaps, more family-friendly than a can of beer.

When held in the hand, a Popsicle is certainly more visible than a canned beverage. In the drawing, the frozen confection is given added prominence through its juxtaposition to the figure's ample belly, which almost obscures the man's swimming trunks.

Powless strengthens the formal composition of the drawing by simplifying the backdrop. The pickup truck has been replaced with a few short horizontal lines suggesting a bench, a beach and a far horizon. A few additional straight lines serve to crop the figure tightly and indicate the edges of the picture frame. Above the frame, in the upper right corner, is a notation from the artist to himself, a reminder to paint the umbrella "lime green and white with lime green shadows" in the final acrylic version. Beneath this notation is the faint outline of an alternate configuration for the hands, with palms facing inwards and fingertips touching. Below the frame, Powless has written in small uppercase letters the words KEEPING COOL. Within the Western art historical tradition, naming a work of art signals a degree of conceptual completion that helps to distinguish an intentionally created image from mere doodling. Within certain Aboriginal traditions, a similar act of naming is believed to breathe life into a subject, thereby bringing it into existence.

*Keeping Cool* exists on its own terms as a drawing, quite apart from the painting it served to inspire. Powless portrays the individual playfully, but with respect and obvious affection, imbuing him with a positive life-force and a wry sense of humour. The man is a memorable presence in a minimal landscape, an (in)active advocate of energy conservation—as a means of keeping cool—on a hot summer's day.

Not long after completing the drawing, Powless painted the much larger version on canvas (see fig. 2). It remains remarkably true to the sketch, in both form and features, but is decidedly different in one respect. The increase in size, coupled with the addition of colour and further detail, renders the image much

*fig. 2:* Indians' Summer, *Bill Powless, acrylic on canvas, 97 × 177 cm, 1984.*

more lifelike and naturalistic, perhaps *too* naturalistic, in its representation of reality. Where the pencil sketch takes pleasure in describing the body's abundant curvature, the painting is far less charitable in depicting so much exposed flesh. Exposed *indigenous* flesh. *Too much* exposed indigenous flesh. Powless confronts, and even startles, viewers with an up-close and intimate portrait of a massive, bronze, red man, who seems at risk

of turning deep orange or salmon pink in the blaze of the midday sun. The notion of a sunburn on such a grand scale hurts the
head. Appearing oblivious to the possible health hazard, the individual savours the moment. (Perhaps he's wearing sunscreen.)
His umbrella headdress is still in place, but now seems incapable
of shading even his eyes, much less offering his body any shelter
from the elements. He is, in large part, clearly exposed.

Following the notation on his drawing, Powless painted the
umbrella with alternating green and white segments. Remi-
niscent of a circus tent, it is anchored with vertical struts to a
pale blue knit sweatband stretching across the man's broad forehead. His hair appears tangled and windswept, matted against
his skin, wet and stringy. His pendant earring is still visible, as
is the lone feather floating on the breeze against the sky. It is
definitely an eagle feather. He is definitely an Indian. Like the
other features in the original drawing, the Popsicle has acquired
further definition on canvas. It is now deep purple in colour,
evoking the sweet taste of grape. It is also dripping, and vaguely
phallic in appearance.

The physical setting for the portrait is more fully realized
as well. Clad only in the briefest of red bathing trunks, the man
rests on the bench of what looks to be a white picnic table. While
this may not be the most comfortable seat, he appears content.
The table is set against a green grassy bank leading down to a
sandy beach, with bright blue water beyond. A fluffy smudge of
cloud sits on the horizon, separating the sky from the water, as
waves break in the distance and roll in to shore.

It is a beautiful day to be indigenous.

In the process of translating the image from pencil to paint,
Powless also reworked the title. The individualistic and descrip-
tive *Keeping Cool* was dropped in favour of the more communal
and metaphoric *Indians' Summer*. The name change reflects
a broader focus that seems appropriate to the increase in size.

The painting is a larger, bolder and more visually public statement than the drawing. To reinforce the expanded reference,
Powless chose the plural possessive noun "Indians'" over the
singular "Indian's." As with some of his other works that bear
deceptively simple titles, *Indians' Summer* invites a range of
interpretive readings.

For example, in general usage, the term "Indian summer" is
understood to be an unexpected yet welcome burst of warmth
in the midst of autumn. It is unclear why this phenomenon is
considered "Indian," but it is a respite meant to be thoroughly
enjoyed. And that is exactly what Powless portrays in this painting: a moment of personal pleasure in the summer sun. Arguably,
one of the primary themes of this work is the simple assertion
that Aboriginal peoples share in the same everyday activities
and recreational pleasures as the non-Aboriginal population.
Why is this surprising? While the painting imagines one individual's experience, the plural possessive noun "Indians'" in the
title suggests that this may be an activity in which other Indians—perhaps whole communities of other Indians—participate
as well. The interpretive possibilities of the possessive title do
not end with imagining communal participation, however, but
in fact allow for an even more radical and intriguing reading—
one of communal *ownership,* of a season, no less! As an assertion of communal ownership, or "Aboriginal title," *Indians'
Summer* functions much like a land claim, only in a temporal
sphere, putting a new twist on the notion of "Indian time" and a
different spin on the concept of "time sharing."

*INDIANS' SUMMER* WAS SHOWN, along with *Fear of Wet Feathers,* another painting by Powless, in Beginnings, an exhibition
of Native art mounted in January 1985 by Hamilton Artists Inc.,
an artist-run gallery in Hamilton, Ontario. A photograph of a
young woman admiring the painting of the big Indian appeared

in the January 19 edition of the *Hamilton Spectator*, alongside a review by arts critic Grace Inglis. In her review, Inglis calls Powless "a pleasurable discovery," describing his pieces as "total delights and well painted too." She writes: "[He] has revealed himself as a painter of hilarious send-ups on the inscrutable Indian, not unkind to his race, but prodding, in none too subtle a fashion, the general image of ceremony and dignity, and pointing out that, really, Indians are just folks underneath all the feathers and paint." In the article, Powless expresses his growing interest in depicting contemporary rather than traditional Indian subject matter. He adds that his colleagues at the Woodland Cultural Centre find his paintings funny, and that no one has been offended. Inglis concludes, "Bill's message is not against tradition, but for [recognition of] the human within the tradition. There are not to be any sacred cows for Bill Powless."

Within a few months of the Hamilton show, *Indians' Summer* was selected as the signature image for Indian Art '85, an exhibition of new works by Aboriginal artists scheduled to open at the Woodland Cultural Centre in May of that year and run for six weeks. Since its modest beginnings in the mid-1970s, the centre's annual art show has become an increasingly important showcase for emerging Native artists, as well as a barometer of new trends in Aboriginal aesthetic expression. The catalogue to the yearly exhibition, which documents all the works and provides context for the show, has become an invaluable resource for researchers. In his curatorial essay for the 1985 catalogue, Museum Director Tom Hill draws attention to a recent increase in the use of satire as a form of social and political commentary. He suggests that it may be part of a developing reactionary movement against a definition of "Indian art" that limits expression to depictions of mythic and heroic themes. *Indians' Summer* was chosen to symbolize this growing oppositional impulse. It was an inspired choice.

Yet Hill presents the painting not so much as an example of resistance or radical redirection but as an innovative exploration of new media, by an artist whose gentle humour was already known to local residents through the illustrations and cartoons he contributed regularly to community and cultural centre publications. The cover of the Indian Art '78 exhibition catalogue, for example, features a pen-and-ink drawing of a mounted warrior wielding a lance-like paintbrush (see fig. 3). The drawing is amusing but not alarming, in the way that *Indians' Summer* is, though it can be argued that both images serve a destabilizing function. Despite the absurd posturing with a giant paintbrush, the mounted brave with the wrapped braids stays firmly in the realm of imagination, whereas the big Indian by the beach threatens to break free of imagination at any moment, and, without moving a muscle, demand a space in the viewer's world.

In the catalogue, Hill describes *Indians' Summer* as "humorous, grotesque and irreverent," and he poses a few questions to help viewers understand this seemingly banal painting of a grossly obese man. For instance, considering its strategic placement in the composition, he asks, Is the melting Popsicle a veiled critique of contemporary Indian culture or a comment on the man's sexuality? Is the painting, in its flagrant reference to and rejection of a romanticized notion of "Indianness," just one more attempt to demystify the Indian artist and his art? And is the use of critical humour a mere passing fad or an expression of a newly discovered cultural confidence? If it is evidence of the latter, and represents the visual transformation of a rich, primarily oral tradition of self-deprecating humour, is it wise to celebrate this transformation in such a public venue, and before an audience of mostly unsuspecting non-Native patrons, who constitute the majority of Indian art consumers? What if they miss the jokes? What if they miss the familiar stereotypes? Hill warns that "being viciously funny for a white audience... is to

*fig. 3: Indian Art '78 exhibition catalogue cover, Bill Powless, pen-and-ink drawing on paper, 1978.*

ask that white [audience] to make judgements and form opinions not only on the art but on the culture as well." While sharing such humour is fraught with risk, it is risk that gives humour its energy and edge. As it turned out, the reactions of white viewers were the least of the gallery's worries.

In the days leading up to the opening, images of *Indians' Summer* seemed to be everywhere. A black-and-white photograph of the painting was used to promote the show in the press, and it was printed on an invitation from the board of governors of the Woodland Cultural Centre to a private preview of the exhibition. Here, the comic spirit of the occasion was nicely captured in the playful juxtaposition of the elegantly scripted formal text with the starkly informal signature image. The monochrome photo was also featured on the cover of the Indian Art '85 catalogue and included inside, along with images of the other works in the show.[1] To complement the catalogue, the centre printed a commemorative poster that reproduced the painting in full colour. This offered viewers an opportunity to bask in the reflected warmth of *Indians' Summer* long after the exhibition closed. Lastly, and in a move that blurs the line between fine art and fine publicity, Powless painted a large version of the poster on plywood, which was then installed at the entrance to the cultural centre, on a main thoroughfare where it could be seen by the many daily commuters travelling to and from Brantford (see fig. 4). It was not long before the media blitz began to generate a response.

Among the more strident reactions was a letter to the editor, printed in the May 29 edition of the Six Nations newspaper *Tekawennake* and signed "An offended Indian." Under the heading "Obese is sick!" it read:

> Art is beautiful in many ways, shapes and forms, but the advertisement for Art '85 falls way short of humour, creativity suitable only for a freak show. I see nothing but disgust every time I see this dumb looking Indian with his belly blown up like a balloon and his boobs hanging and this stupid umbrella hat on his head. The Indians through the years have been stereotyped as being fat, lazy, illiterate and just plain stupid, even in cartoons. In conclusion, what is this artist trying to prove? This is 1985, the human body is beautiful but obese is sick.

*fig. 4: Bill Powless, with acrylic-on-plywood version of Indian Art '85 poster, Woodland Cultural Centre, 1991. Photo by Allan J. Ryan.*

On June 5, Tom Hill wrote a lengthy and considered response to both the headline and the "offended Indian," recapping many of the points he presented in his catalogue essay and expanding on others. It was a necessary gesture, since the essay provided context for the exhibition only, not for the advertisement. With no warning, and no criteria for appreciating the symbolism or the artist's intention, viewers could well be forgiven for respond-

ing with anger. In his letter, Hill agrees that "Obese is sick," but
he does not engage in a discussion of Aboriginal health issues.
Instead, he affirms Powless's credentials as a maker of "original
works of art" and summarizes the circumstances leading up to
the creation of the painting and its subsequent inclusion in the
exhibition. He admits that the artist may have exaggerated certain aspects of the portrait of this "Indian gentleman" in order
to raise important questions. (Hill refers to the individual twice
as a "gentleman," never allowing him or his image to slip into
caricature or cartoon, or to become an object of ridicule.)

Again, Hill suggests that this "grotesque and irreverent"
painting may be asking viewers to consider whether contemporary Aboriginal culture has deteriorated to a set of kitschy
Indian symbols, and whether negative stereotypes created by
non-Indians have been so internalized by Native peoples that
they have difficulty recognizing or accepting reflections of reality. It is somewhat ironic that, as evidence of the latter, Hill says
some Indian viewers are convinced that the individual in the
painting is holding a beer bottle and not a melting Popsicle. (Perhaps they were on the beach with Powless on Manitoulin!) Hill
goes on to praise contemporary Aboriginal artists in general for
daring to go beyond "pointless images of Indians in Sioux war
bonnets riding off into the sunset" to create works that are rich
in ideas and inventiveness, and that are bringing their creators
international acclaim. In defending the artist's right to por-
tray realities which are not always beautiful, he cites Picasso's
anti-war painting *Guernica*, which, when first displayed, was
considered so full of disturbing images and ideas that the artist fled the country for fear of his life. While not endangered to
the same degree, Powless is clearly keeping good company, and
Hill commends him for documenting the constantly changing
shape and face of contemporary Indian culture. In an effort to
silence the critics once and for all, the museum director closes

his letter with a calculated one-two punch, noting that Powless "sold the original painting to a prominent art collector in Ottawa, and the Indian Art '85 poster was the most sought-after poster at the most recent Canadian Museum Association conference in Toronto. The poster is now a collector's item."

Curiously missing from Hill's rejoinder was any mention of humour and satire, the very qualities that the *Hamilton Spectator* critic found so refreshing and that prompted Hill in his catalogue essay to single out the painting as a symbol of shifting artistic currents. Then again, it could be that the omission was deliberate. Clearly, the "offended Indian" was lacking in humour, so it may have seemed pointless to praise the painting for its spirited sense of wry whimsy. Still, it would have been beneficial for other readers to have heard such an argument.

A week after Hill's letter appeared in *Tekawennake,* the well-known Iroquois artist R.G. (Gary) Miller was also prompted to respond to the words of the "offended Indian." He pulled no punches in his energetic rebuke, calling the writer's comparisons of *Indians' Summer* to a freak side show "utterly ridiculous" and denouncing the writer's limited knowledge of both art and physiology. Miller said, in part:

> The artfulness of some self-ordained critics in my opinion shows a stupidity that is only superceded by the fact that this critic is a bigot. Obese people can't always control their pituitary or thyroid glands, hence the weight problem (if you see weight as a problem). The painting is well executed, honest in its portrayal and it conjures profound thought. Of course Indians wish to be portrayed as noble, perfect beings but the fact is we are not. I, for example, have nose hair that's too long; my breath could strip paint etc., etc. On the other hand, we should have the self-assuredness to be able to see ourselves as we are (from the ideal to the depths of human

despair). The artist must make statements that can't please everyone, or indeed anyone, from time to time. If he succeeds in provoking thought then his painting is valid. We are, after all, no better, no worse, than anyone else. Indeed, to some "thin is in," to others, "fat's where it's at." Bill, I bow to your achievement. Your painting is honest, humorous, satirical and it shows we too have human frailties. The majority of us will view it in the good taste in which it is intended.

P.S. Does the "Offended Indian" insinuate that we artists should tolerate such impertinence from a mere microscopic spec of animosity? Well, do you?

In conversation a few years later, Hill recalled that there was a lot more public response to the painting than what was reported in the newspaper: "There were calls to our board of governors. I met with people here [at the museum] in person. There was a great deal of concern that maybe the piece was perpetuating the stereotype—an unflattering stereotype. I was quite surprised!"[2] Powless, too, was surprised: "The Indians on the reserve here didn't like it at all," he remembers. "My son got called down. The kids were telling him that their mother and dad didn't like it [because] it made people think all Indians were fat. It was like they wanted the stereotype of the noble warrior, slim and trim and nothing else." Powless added that the poster of the painting was hung in the local seniors' home to remind residents of what they did *not* want to look like.[3]

Given the widespread apprehension, how *did* non-Natives respond to the painting? As the artist put it, after observing those who visited the centre and saw the work displayed in the gallery, "They weren't sure whether to laugh or not. Some people just broke out [in laughter], they couldn't help it, and some people weren't sure whether they were supposed to laugh or not. I could see them trying to hold it back."

For both Native and non-Native viewers, the ghost of the noble warrior remains a forceful presence in *Indians' Summer*, haunting the canvas and clinging to the figure like an invisible cloak, provoking ripples of nervous laughter and sometimes anger. This peculiar double vision exemplifies the power of critical parody. *Indians' Summer* is a wickedly subversive parody of the numerous historic portraits of indigenous war chiefs and peacemakers who posed, resplendent in their beaded and feathered finery, for non-Native painters (and later photographers) who sought to fix their subjects' images in public memory before they vanished from the cultural and physical landscape, along with the rest of their ill-fated race. The demise of indigenous people was said to be imminent.

In *Indians' Summer*, Powless visually invokes, then quickly inverts, many of the symbols and assumptions associated with this urgent project of cultural salvage. The painting's insistence on doubleness is relentless: the proud warrior's once trim physique has ballooned to alarming proportions, his familiar leather loincloth has been replaced with a pair of skimpy bathing trunks, his telltale beaded headband is now a trendy yuppie sweatband and his flowing feathered headdress is but a mundane shade of its former glory. Gone but not forgotten are the well-known markers of spiritual and military power: the quilled pipestem, the feathered fan and the decorated hatchet. In their stead is an ice-water confection, melting in the midday sun. As I have noted elsewhere, "Despite such comic turns and transformations, a basic human dignity, even nobility, still abides. Divested of all manner of exotic trappings, this self-satisfied image of contemporary reality gently confounds the viewer and all but demolishes romantic fantasy."[4]

TWO DECADES have now elapsed since Powless first ruffled the sensibilities of local residents with his brazen image of inflated Indianness, challenging viewers to reconsider the complex rela-

*fig. 5:* "So…what do you think…," *Bill Powless, pen-and-ink cartoon on paper, 1989.*

tionship between cultural and artistic practice. Powless continues to paint and to oversee the design of exhibitions and publications at the Woodland Cultural Centre.[5] It has also been two decades since Hill questioned whether the zealous embrace of satire by indigenous artists was a passing fad—a momentary flirtation with the mannerisms of postmodern irony—or the visual manifestation of a gathering Aboriginal awareness and confidence. Time has clearly shown it to be the latter, with critical satire merely one of many aesthetic strategies deployed by indigenous artists to interrogate history and illuminate contemporary experience. Yet just a few of these artists demonstrate a true mastery of the light touch and the quick getaway. Their work is all the more memorable for its rarity.[6]

— NOTES —

1. The show also includes *Beer Garden*, a second painting by Powless from 1984. Interpreting the title literally rather than metaphorically, the artist depicts two men at work in the garden, one scattering beer bottle caps on the ground, in the manner of Johnny Appleseed, while the other tills the soil with a hoe. Above them, a sequence of time-lapse images illustrates how the bottle caps take root and grow into mature bottles of beer ready for harvest. It is not the standard media coupling of Indians and alcohol.

Powless created one other painting in 1984 that deserves mention, though it was not included in the Indian Art '85 show. In what might be considered a comic variation on a theme, *Beach Blanket Brave* is an accurate portrayal of the familiar "Indian warrior" stereotype, that is, a strapping male figure be-feathered, bemused and looking suitably stoic. An admirable specimen of indigenous manhood, he stands on the shoreline wrapped in a large beach towel, sporting a trendy Speedo bathing suit and clutching a newspaper and a rubber inner tube. The painting was exhibited in Art of the Seventh Generation: Iroquois Symbols on Canvas and Paper at the Roberson Center for the Arts and Sciences, Binghamton, New York, May–July 1986. A black-and-white photograph of the piece appears in the catalogue to the show, and also in this writer's book, *The Trickster Shift: Humour and Irony in Contemporary Native Art*, Vancouver and Seattle: UBC Press and University of Washington Press, 1999, p. 16.

Indian Art '85 also introduced the public to Carl Beam's *The North American Iceberg*, a large and important mixed-media on Plexiglas work, whose satirical title referenced the exhibition The European Iceberg, which had recently visited Toronto. The following year, in what was to become a watershed moment in the history of institutional collecting in Canada, the piece was purchased by the National Gallery of Canada, becoming the first work by a Canadian Aboriginal artist to be acquired by the gallery in over sixty years.

2. Personal conversation, October 1, 1991, quoted in *The Trickster Shift*, p. 57.

3. Personal conversation, February 11, 1991, quoted in *The Trickster Shift*, p. 57.

4. *The Trickster Shift*, p. 55. In 1989, five years after completing *Indians' Summer*, Powless submitted a cartoon to *Tekawennake* that featured a stereotypic Indian brave in the role of a generic Indian Everyman, wearing the distinctive umbrella headpiece (see fig. 5).

5. His 1995 painting *Abracadabra (I'm Gonna Reach Up and Grab Ya!)*, a wry depiction of a tricky politician as a midway magician, was a highlight of the 1998 exhibition Iroquois Art: Visual Expressions of Contemporary Native American Artists at the Amerika Haus, Frankfurt am Main, Germany. See the catalogue to the exhibition, edited by Sylvia Kasprycki, co-published by the *European Review of Native American Studies* and University of Washington Press (Seattle, WA), 1998, pp. 93–94.

6. Among the most accomplished practitioners, in addition to Powless: Jeff Thomas, Rosalie Favell, Ron Noganosh, Edward Poitras, Shelley Niro, Brian Jungen, Gerald McMaster, Jim Logan, Lawrence Paul Yuxweluptun, Teresa Marshall, Greg Hill, Kent Monkman and Riel Benn.

# TEASING,
# TOLERATING, TEACHING

............................

### LAUGHTER *and* COMMUNITY *in*
### NATIVE *Literature*

.............

### { KRISTINA FAGAN }

**P**OMO-MIWOK WRITER Greg Sarris begins his collection of essays on Native literature, *Keeping Slug Woman Alive*, with a joke at his own expense. He describes himself, a Stanford graduate student, sitting at his aunt's kitchen table and taking notes on his relatives' conversation. Soon he was ordered by his aunt to put down the notebook and help her peel potatoes. In a nervous attempt to make his potatoes as smooth and as round as hers, he peeled and peeled, shaving off every rough spot:

> I set my knife down and leaned back in my chair, just for a
> moment, just to let Aunt Violet know I was finished. But she
> was not moving. Her face was tight, swollen, blushed with
> color, her eyes set on her pile of peelings where she held her
> knife, pointing. The peelings, something I hadn't thought

of... Her peelings were paper thin, shards of skin, thinner than carrot peelings, almost transparent. I felt the thick, coarse lumps under my hand. I lifted my eyes just in time to catch Auntie Violet hiss. "Just like a white man," she managed to say, exploding with laughter. "So wasteful!" The entire room was laughing.[1]

Virtually all of the scholarly writing on humour in Aboriginal literature examines the ways in which Aboriginal writers use humour to subvert white society and to counter colonization and stereotypes. We could take this approach to Sarris's story, pointing out that Auntie Violet is criticizing the wastefulness and excess of the dominant society and also, perhaps, indirectly scolding Sarris for behaving like a (white) anthropologist towards his own family. However, to read Aboriginal humour only in terms of its relationship to white society is limiting. As Thomas King has pointed out, such readings can "make it sound as though the Native people spend their entire existence fighting against non-Native whatever. That just isn't true."[2] If we look at Sarris's story from another angle, we can see that it tells us a great deal about how he wants us to see him and his own community. With this story, he begins his study not by establishing his authority but by demonstrating just how much he does not know. Rather than asserting individual expertise, Sarris is establishing the value that he places on indigenous community knowledge. By making himself an object of ridicule, he subordinates his position to the communal values represented by his elder, Auntie Violet. The incident also brings to light his struggle, as a mixed-blood Native person raised in foster homes, to fit into his own communal ideal.

Aboriginal writers often use humour, as Sarris does here, in depicting the complex inner workings of Aboriginal communities. In fact, numerous writers and critics have asserted that humour has been the key to Aboriginal communities' survival. Lakota scholar Vine Deloria, for instance, writes, "When a people can laugh at themselves and laugh at others and hold all aspects of life together without letting anyone drive them to extremes, then it would seem to me that the people can survive."[3] But few people have elaborated on the process through which laughter leads to community survival. So, in this essay, I explore how several Aboriginal authors depict the social functions of humour within Aboriginal communities. These writers are aware that "community" is neither an ideal nor a fixed thing. Rather, a Native community is continually being built and challenged, and humour can play a role in both these processes. On the one hand, humour is deeply social: a shared laugh is an affirmation of norms, attitudes and assumptions in common. Humour can allow the tolerance of disruptive forces, teach social values and enforce social norms. But these functions can have a problematic side, sometimes leaving people feeling excluded or humiliated, as happens in Sarris's story. Thus, Native writers also use humour not only to shore up community but also to complicate and problematize it.

Most often, however, humour helps to create social harmony within communities. This has traditionally made it an important tool in the lives of Aboriginal people. Especially when most Native people lived primarily in small, family-based groups, group cohesion was essential. Mohawk psychiatrist Clare Brant explains:

> The individual and group survival of this continent's aboriginal Plains, Bush, and Woodlands people required harmonious interpersonal relationships and cooperation among members of a group. It was not possible for an individual to survive alone in the harsh natural environment but, in order to survive as a group, individuals, living cheek by jowl throughout their lives, had to be continuously cooperative and friendly.[4]

Today, this group harmony remains necessary in the face of the many threats, mostly human rather than environmental, to Native communities. This harmony has been maintained in part by suppressing conflict.[5] And laughter has been an effective tool in this suppression, defusing or sublimating tension and negativity.

You will notice, as you read this essay, that the characters who use this socially cohesive humour are often elders. Breaking the stereotype of the stately and dignified old Indian, these characters laugh at themselves and others. This joking role is an indication of the respect and authority that elders are accorded in Native communities. Métis educator Fyre Jean Graveline explains that elders' humour plays a key role in maintaining community balance:

> "Too much of one thing can lead to imbalance," "Don't take life so seriously," "Don't make yourself bigger than you really are," my Elders taught. Too much power and too much seriousness are feared, for they can unbalance life in the Community and the environment.[6]

Some younger comedians have used the joking power of elders to their advantage. In their comedy stage show, the young Tlingit and Tutchone actors Sharon Shorty and Jackie Bear perform as elders, telling irreverent stories and demanding audience participation. Similarly, Mohawk ventriloquist Buddy Big Mountain uses an "elder puppet" to make the jokes in his act. Many writers also place the figure of the humorous elder at the centre of their representations of community.

One of the most common ways Native writers represent humour is as a means of coping. Humour is shown as offering a sense of relief and an acceptance of circumstance in the face of danger or tragedy. Gerald Vizenor describes this comic perspective:

You're never striving for anything that is greater than life itself. There's an acceptance of chance. Sometimes things just happen and when they happen, even though they may be dangerous or even life threatening, there is some humor… And it's a positive, compassionate act of survival, it's getting along.[7]

An anthropologist who spent time among the Netsilik Inuit provides a striking example of this accepting humour. She tells of a Netsilik man whose house and belongings were destroyed in a storm and describes how she stood and watched in astonishment as this man laughed heartily about his fate. When she asked her informants how the man could laugh under such circumstances, they explained that, had the man yelled or cried, he would have alienated and embarrassed the others in the village. However, by showing his good humour, he was more likely to receive help from others in rebuilding his house.[8] By laughing at his problems, the man relieved social tensions and maintained the sense of solidarity that was necessary to his own survival.

In his play *fareWel*, Ian Ross depicts this accepting and comic perspective through the character called "Nigger." Nigger, an elder, is portrayed as the centre of the "Partridge Crop Reserve," representing the key to the people's endurance. At first glance, Nigger may seem to be lacking as a model for community survival; he is most funny when getting injured—hit by a truck, bitten by a dog, shot, or chewed by a chainsaw. He moves passively and genially through the events of the play, never taking a side in the political arguments that dominate the plot, certainly never being the stereotypically sage elder. Instead, he plays the hapless bum, looking only for a cigarette and a free meal.

Nigger is neither an interpreter nor a teacher within his community. It matters little to him whether events make sense. When he reads a comic strip in French and doesn't understand it, he laughs anyway. He rarely gives advice, and when he does, it is never from a position of authority. For instance, when advising Melvin not to sniff gas, Nigger says, "That sniffing's no good. I caught fire the time I tried it."[9] However, Native people have traditionally learned by "observing and feeling" what their elders do rather than by direct instruction.[10] In the poverty and unrest of the Partridge Crop Reserve, Nigger's generous, tolerant and undefeatable comic attitude is an essential model. In fact, his attitude informs the very structure of the play.

Despite all the problems on the reserve, Ross does not structure his story as a tragedy. Instead, he takes, like Nigger, a comic view of reserve politics. The choice between the comic and the tragic view of reserve life is made explicit in a conversation between Nigger and a younger woman, Rachel. In this conversation, Nigger criticizes his own survival tactics, saying that he is not a good man because he is not dead: people, he says, "only talk good about you when you're dead."[11] Nigger is describing a tragic world view, one that has simultaneously idealized Native people and presented them as a tragic and dying race. Rachel, however, responds to this by affirming Nigger's comic survival response to the world: "You're a good man, Sheldon [Nigger]... 'Cause you don't die."[12] In the same way, the Partridge Crop community is presented as good because it does not die. The play has a classic comic ending, with the characters coming together in their acceptance of each other and the reserve. This ending allows the audience to feel good about the Partridge Crop Reserve. The play asks us to adopt Nigger's attitude: focus on the ridiculous, avoid anger or sadness, and keep going.

Ross's depiction of Nigger, however, also shows the limits of this comic perspective. Our laughter alleviates some of the tensions that the play raises about the high death rate on reserves and the touchy issue of self-government. But at the end these tensions remain, and the illness, hunger and poverty depicted in the play remain unchanged. We are left wondering if "not dying" is a sufficient goal in life. We get the sense that, with Nigger's approach, the community will survive but will not change. Does the maintenance of community require such a conservative outlook?

Perhaps the coping humour used by Nigger, while not itself a force of change, opens up psychological space for future change to take place. This further step is shown in Ruby Slipperjack's novel *Honour the Sun*. Like Ross, Slipperjack uses humour to emphasize the closeness of a small Native community. In her novel, laughter often revolves around the escapades of a clumsy, clown-like character who is identified only as "the Town Joker." Unlike Nigger, the Town Joker uses laughter to inspire resistance as well as acceptance in the face of danger. For the young protagonist, Owl, and her family, which is headed by a single mother, the greatest danger comes from the drunken men who sometimes wander through the village breaking into cabins. Just after such a drunk has shot the family dog, the Joker makes his first appearance in the novel, tickling people, slipping on fish guts and generally causing a ruckus. In another incident, a drunken intruder catches and assaults Owl's mother. But the next morning the Town Joker shows up, falling clumsily through the door that was broken the night before, and the chapter suddenly changes tone, dissolving into slapstick. Owl falls off her toboggan, her brother tears the seat of his pants and the chapter ends with the family sitting around teasing one another. They have not called the police; nor have they "worked through" the previous night's trauma. And yet the Joker's perpetual silliness turns the situation around. He also literally turns things around, helping the mother to build a door that can be barred from the inside. Owl calls it "a backwards door. Whoever heard of a door opening backwards?"[13] Such reversal occurs often in Native "transformation stories": "The physical characteristics of this domain are the reverse of those found in the more familiar world... This view of human social order is not a mirror image, but one that (like myth itself) simultaneously unbalances and reorients the protagonist, revealing the ordinary in new ways."[14] Of course, the reversal of norms is also a common element in humour. So the "backwards door," representing transformation, humour and a very practical means of fighting back, becomes an appropriate symbol of the Town Joker's role.

The Joker's gift of laughter even seems able to prevent disaster. On Christmas night, the Joker arrives, teasing the mother incessantly. He leaves again, and the family is still giggling about his jokes when the man who had assaulted Owl's mother crashes through the door. This time, however, they attack him with a broom and pieces of firewood until he runs away. Owl describes the family's response after the incident:

> I sigh as I feel my body relax. Then, a slow pressure builds in my chest and I begin to giggle. Still standing around by the stove, they all look at me. Then they, too, start to laugh. That is all I need; I let my laughter go. Oh, that was so good to see. I feel like hugging them all.[15]

In this scene, the family faces challenges and laughs together, showing their shared perspective and collective strength.

In a sense, both Nigger and the Town Joker are community teachers, though they never do offer instruction or criticism. In some other works, humour is shown being used in a more overtly educational way. However, even when a joke or humorous story is offered as educational, it is rarely interpreted. This reticence is in keeping with traditional Native educational practices, which generally discourage direct instruction as inappropriate interference. Stories and jokes encourage people to observe and interpret on their own, allowing them to see multiple possible meanings. Laughter also makes the teaching seem less pushy and coercive and shows that the teacher is not arrogant or self-important. Vi Hilbert, a Salish historian, remembers her own childhood experience of listening to stories from her elders: "While the stories were told to me in great detail, allowing for my delicate ears, the moral was never, ever explained to me."[16] Barre Toelken, in a discussion of Navajo Trickster tales, points out that this indirection does not mean there is no teaching taking place:

> [The humour] functions as a way of directing the responses of the audience vis à vis significant moral factors. Causing children to laugh at an action because it is thought to be weak, stupid or excessive is to order their moral assessment of it without recourse to open explanation or didacticism.[17]

Here, though, Toelken somewhat oversimplifies the teaching function of humour. It is rare for humour to simply demonstrate unsuitable behaviour. Instead, humour tends to indirectly explore troublesome or contradictory areas of life. There are usually many possible "lessons" condensed in a joke, none of which represent *the* lesson.

As an example of the multiple meanings that can be carried in a seemingly simple humorous story, consider the traditional Innu story of how Wolverine got stuck in Bear's skull. Wolverine is a born survivor—an indomitable and self-sufficient hunter, much like the traditional Innu.[18] However, he often makes a mess of things. In this story, Wolverine is famished, having eaten only lemmings and shrews for a long time. He tricks Bear by pretending to be her brother and then kills her. He has a craving for Bear's brain, so he transforms himself into a maggot, enters Bear's skull through the eye socket and feasts. But when he has finished eating, he discovers that he is too fat to escape the skull. By the time he is thin enough to crawl back out, the rest of the meat has been eaten by other animals.[19] So Wolverine must continue his hunt for food, hungry once again.

The humour of this story works in many directions. The fear and reality of being hungry is something that is familiar to northern Native peoples, and Wolverine's situation revolves around this troublesome issue. On the one hand, the listener can identify with Wolverine's hunger, admire his cunning in overcoming it and laugh at the easily duped Bear. But Wolverine is also a target of laughter. His behaviour in the story is inappropriate and he gets his comeuppance. While hunters need to kill animals, hunting is a process that traditionally involves cooperation between the spirits of hunter and hunted: the spirit of the hunted animal must give permission for its body to be killed. The way in which Wolverine kills Bear is dishonest and therefore immoral. The story also warns against Wolverine's greed and impatience, qualities that ultimately leave him hungry again. But again, listeners can identify with and take pleasure in Wolverine's adaptability and survival skills in escaping Bear's skull. And Wolverine is able to shrug off his mistakes and keep going—an important lesson. Clearly the Innu audience's responses to this story would be complex, multiple and divided. The troublesome issue of how to morally respond to hunger is condensed but not settled.

Humour is also used in written Native literature as a complex teaching tool. For example, Louise Halfe's *Bear Bones & Feathers* and Gregory Scofield's *I Knew Two Metis Women* both depict the humorous teachings of Native mothers, grandmothers and aunts. These elders use humour to teach mixed and ambiguous lessons about life. The women themselves are much like Wolverine, both foolish and wise, both role models and warnings. Scofield's poetry collection is a tribute to his mother and "Aunty" (a family friend), their love of country music, their raucous humour and their gutsy attitude. Aunty especially uses humour to teach the young Gregory. Early in the collection, Scofield describes how she taught him to count in Cree by counting incorrectly, prompting him to correct her with "Keeskwiyan [You're crazy]."[20] Throughout, Aunty continues to teach by humorously playing up her own faults. But her humour becomes darker and more edgy as the book progresses. She lived a short disordered life, full of music and laughter but also marked by violence, poverty, alcohol and abuse. Her humour acknowledges that life, celebrates it and warns against it. Scofield describes how she told him about beating up three women in a bar:

> She looks up, mischievous
> As Wesakeejak
> Spinning his tall tales.
> "Tapway [It's true]," she grins,
> "No wooman mess around wit me."
>
> "Ah, mucheementow [devil]," I scold
> To her laughter,
>
> Though growing up
> How many times I wished she'd come to school,
> Hand-talk the bully.[21]

In another incident, Aunty gives her common-law husband a black eye. "Aunt-ee," Scofield protests, "No wonder he brought the cops."[22] But when police arrive, it is the husband who is arrested for domestic abuse. Scofield recounts Aunty making blueberry bannock to take him in jail: "'Blue bannock for dah blue eye,' she chuckled, heading out the door. 'Dah bugger will like dat.'"[23] Scofield admires and longs for his aunt's survival and fighting skills, but his repeated scolding also shows that he identifies her behaviour as inappropriate. She is both kind and unkind, capable and incapable, honest and dishonest. There is no clear moral lesson in her jokes, but rather moral dilemmas that push in various directions.

The speaker in Louise Halfe's *Bear Bones & Feathers* describes her mother in similar terms, also describing her as

"Wesahkecahk," whose "pleurisy mocks [her] laughter."[24] She, like Aunty, experiences domestic violence, carrying "ghosts of blueberry shiners / and an arm glazed in strawberry stains."[25] The speaker describes her mother's teachings about "body politics":

> Mama said,
>
> Real women
> don't steal
> from the sky and wear clouds
> on their eyelids.
>
> Real women
> eat rabbit well-done
> not left half-raw
> on their mouth...
>
> When she was finished talking
> she clicked her teeth
> lifted her arse
> and farted
> at the passing
> city women.[26]

Halfe, throughout her collection, celebrates women's comfort with their own bodies, a comfort here embodied in the speaker's mother. And yet the mother also wears blue on her eyes and red on her mouth, from beatings rather than from makeup. Clearly, there is an irony in the mother's concept of a real woman; again, her humour both teaches and warns.

Maggie-the-Fox in Tomson Highway's *Kiss of the Fur Queen* offers a message that could perhaps sum up the philosophy of Scofield's Aunty, Halfe's mother, Ross's Nigger and many other characters in Native literature:

> "We dance, we fight, we cry, make love, we laugh and work
>     and play, we die. Then we wake up, in the dressing room,

with make-up all over the goddamn place, sweating so you
smell like dog's crotch. I mean, get over it, Alice. You ain't
got much time before that grand finale. So you get your little Cree ass out there. Just don't come here wastin' my time
going, 'Oh, boo-hoo-hoo-hoo, poor me, oh, boo.'"[27]

At first it may seem that Fox's philosophy is the "moral" of Highway's novel; she, in her various forms, is with the characters
from birth to death, representing their link to their family and
spirituality. However, while Highway celebrates Fox's survival
spirit, his novel can also be read as a warning against the uncon-
trolled indulgence she represents, whether in sex, alcohol or art.
And she is strongly associated with various female characters
that appear fleetingly throughout the novel, characters who are
often drunk and abused.

Wolverine and Fox, like Scofield's Aunty and Halfe's mother,
are central to the representation of Native community in the
works in which they appear. As traditional figures or elders,
they have a long connection to the community and have gained
knowledge through experience. And yet, we are left to puzzle
over what they can tell us about their communities. In all of
these examples, the comic characters embody excess, enjoyment, rule-breaking and disorderliness. At the same time, there
is also a sense of moral and social order being asserted in each
situation. This contradiction is the source of the humour. But
it is also a deeply social contradiction; the point at which these
forces meet is the fine edge between individual freedom and
communal norms. This is an edge that each of us must negotiate,
a process that is reflected (and perhaps learned) in our negotiation of this teaching humour.

Of course, this negotiation is never simple and can be painful. Thus far, I have emphasized the ways in which humour is
depicted as a non-coercive and harmonious means of maintaining and enforcing community. But the truth is, as Native

writers show us, that despite its innocent appearance humour revolves around the heterogeneity, conflict and complexity of social life. Thus, while humour can reinforce social cohesion, the flip side of this is that it can be used to pressure people into such cohesion. Community depends on a degree of conformity, and humour can be a way of establishing conformity without openly revealing deep negative emotions and without directly criticizing, blaming or interfering with others, thus maintaining social harmony. Joseph Bruchac writes that Native humour is used to keep all community members on the same level: "Humor can be used to remind people—who because of their achievements might be feeling a little too proud or important— that they are no more valuable than anyone else in the circle of life. Teasing someone who gets a little too 'tall' may help shrink them back to the right height."[28] Vine Deloria further explains the teasing process:

> Rather than embarrass members of the tribe publicly, people used to tease individuals they considered out of step with the consensus of tribal opinion. In this way egos were preserved and disputes within the tribe... were held to a minimum.[29]

A striking real-life example of the use of teasing as a social control can be found in Jean-Guy Goulet's study of the Dene Tha, *Ways of Knowing*. Goulet recounts the experiences of a young Dene man named Paul. The Dene Tha believe in the reincarnation of souls, and Paul had always been told that he was the reincarnation of a young girl named Denise; he and his community recognized him as being both a man and a woman. However, as Paul grew up, he was pressured to break with his female side. He was finally, in his late twenties, pushed into proving his masculine identity by having sex with a young woman. Goulet recounts:

For a week or so after the event, Paul was constantly teased in public, in the store, at church, on the road, with people asking him in Dené Dháh if he had enjoyed himself. Paul would inevitably laugh with them, acknowledging that the experience had, indeed, taken place and it had given him much pleasure.[30]

Paul has been pushed to take his place in the normative Dene social order. Though Goulet doesn't mention it, the story does leave me wondering whether Paul might have preferred a homosexual, bisexual or transsexual identity (or perhaps a gender role for which we have no English label). Perhaps the constant teasing of Paul, however affectionate, is ultimately oppressive. The community repeatedly reminds Paul of his female identity in order to shut that identity down. However, while it maintains social order, the teasing does have another side. It keeps the existence of Paul's double identity in people's minds, maintaining it as a possibility.

Many Native writers use this double function of teasing in their writing. Through their depiction of teasing, they can both show community norms and remind us of the limits of and resistance to these norms. For instance, in her poem "Fireflies," Métis poet Marilyn Dumont vividly describes how the speaker's elders use laughter to pressure her into finding a man and taking on her "proper" heterosexual role:

> The old women cup their hankies in their sinew hands and giggle and tease like mosquitoes buzzing around my head and they ask 'what does he eat in winter?' I look blank faced and earnest and say 'I don't know,' and they slap their knees and burst into laughter, talking in Cree... They talk fast, banter and stifle their cackles and ask 'whether he has teeth left and which ones are left,' and they snort into their hands like insufferable children and one of them tells a story and

they all shake like fools with laughter and straighten their
scarves on their heads and pull their skirts over their knees
that bob like ducks in water. They make more tea and laugh
and I know that they do this because they know better and
because they have met more fireflies.[31]

The "fireflies" are the men who will lead the speaker into her
"hottest flame."[32] As she says, the old women "know better" than
their own jokes, recognizing the difficulties and perils of relationships between men and women (difficulties that Dumont's
collection depicts). In fact, she says, they laugh *because* of this
knowledge, suggesting that perhaps the less normative, less
ordered knowledge that underlies such teasing is what gives it
its humorous edge. But teasing still allows the women to, without giving direct advice, push the speaker towards the normative and, the poem suggests, ultimately satisfying world of wives
and mothers.

Like Dumont's poem, Slipperjack's *Honour the Sun* ultimately affirms community norms. However, it also shows that
fitting into such norms can be difficult. I earlier described how,
in the novel, the Town Joker's teasing is a source of together-
ness and strength. However, as Owl gets older, teasing becomes
a means of keeping her in line. Owl describes a humiliating
day during which she is repeatedly the butt of her community's
jokes. In each incident, the laughter of others communicates to
Owl that she must grow up and conform. First, Owl is sitting
on a beach looking at a piece of driftwood when her friend Joe,
whom she herself has recently teased because of his changing
voice, approaches her:

> Then this weird low voice comes out of his mouth. "What are
> you doing? And don't laugh!" he orders.
> I look up at him for a second. "Oh, I'm just trying to see a
> figure of an animal's head or something in this," I said.

He chuckles, "Looks like the thing between a man's legs to me."

I jump up, really mad now, "You get out of here!"[33]

Here, Joe is initiating a more grown-up relationship between him and the unwilling Owl. This incident pushes Owl towards the adult world of sexual undertones and possibilities that will dominate the latter part of the novel. Later that day, Owl is scolded by her mother for carrying a slingshot:

> "They say as long as a girl can stretch a slingshot, that's how long her tits will be!" There's a sudden explosion of choking and giggling all around the table. "I don't have it anymore. I already threw it away..." my voice fades away.[34]

Here, sexual teasing is again used to change Owl's behaviour, in this case to urge her towards acceptable female behaviour. Finally, Owl is laughed at by friends and family when she mistakes a bearskin for a dead dog. She rushes home, tearing her shirt in her impatience, and blurts out, "Hey Mom! Know the old man over there that owns that old, black dog? He's floating dead in the water at the beach!"[35] Her mother looks at her and says, "The old man or the old dog?"[36] Owl's mistake is quickly discovered, and her mother's laughter punishes her for being unobservant, impulsive and excitable. By showing the ways in which Owl is pressured to fulfill expectations, Slipperjack reinforces our sense that the character belongs to a coherent community. At the same time, Owl's embarrassment and resistance to this teasing continually reminds us of the ways in which she does not fit within those expectations.

As Slipperjack shows us, the full realization of community is impossible. There will always be threats to a community's coherence: ideas that are different or people who do not fit in. The differences that prevent the achievement of a completely unified community can be piled on a scapegoat, the victim of humour. Slipperjack is alert to the potentially negative consequences of teasing, to what James English calls "the peculiar double-edgedness of this process, to the violent exclusionism on which the warm vision of community depends."[37]

Haisla writer Eden Robinson explores more extensively than Slipperjack does the aggression and exclusion that can be involved in teasing. In Robinson's short story "Contact Sports," the teenaged Jeremy uses teasing to harass and torture his cousin Tom. He constantly teases Tom about his looks, his sexuality and his epilepsy, and he then downplays these put-downs, saying that they are just jokes: "Just ragging you, kid."[38] In Jeremy's actions, we can see the distortion of the gently educational humour seen in previous examples. As the older of the two, Jeremy seizes the role of the teasing elder and forces Tom to conform to his standards, making him cut his hair and wear different clothing. Tom's "makeover" is, in Jeremy's eyes, a "joke"—causing Tom to be ridiculed at school. Jeremy tries to justify his controlling behaviour as a sign of his affection and his connectedness, saying Tom is like his brother. However, Tom is not permitted to return this kind of humour, as he discovers when he splashes Jeremy with a hose and is immediately threatened.[39] The act of joking is presented as an effort to grab power, and Jeremy wishes to possess all the power in their relationship. Jeremy confirms his position as an aggressive joker by tickling Tom. Tom is forced to laugh until "his ribs felt bruised and he was panting heavily, almost crying."[40] Being tickled, a mixture of laughter and powerlessness, is representative of Tom's experiences throughout the story.

"Contact Sports" raises disturbing questions about the power relations involved in humour. In fact, the title itself points to the pleasure humans seem to take in someone else's pain, especially if that pain is part of a game, a "sport" or a joke. All of the examples discussed in this essay involve some form of emotional pain, and often physical violence. Nigger is punched in the face and the Town Joker repeatedly falls down. Wolverine is starving and Fox is abused. Scofield's Aunty and Halfe's mother are involved in domestic violence, and Owl and Tom are humiliated. In every case, humour is entwined with and implicated in violence and ridicule. And these are only a few of many possible examples. Consider, for instance, the many hilarious and hurtful insults in Tomson Highway's *The Rez Sisters* and in Drew Hayden Taylor's *alter*natives, Maria Campbell's recollections of childish humiliations in *Halfbreed* and the adolescent taunting in Richard Van Camp's *The Lesser Blessed*.

It may be surprising to realize that there is a pattern of violence and humiliation in these works, since most of them create a warm image of Native families and communities talking and laughing together. Furthermore, I have emphasized the importance of harmony within Native societies—an emphasis that does not seem to fit with such a disturbing pattern. It is tempting to say that since the violence occurs within the realm of humour it is, as Jeremy argues, "just a joke." In a sense, this is true. The humour in these works does not permanently harm anybody. Nigger may fall down but he gets up again, and Owl may feel humiliated but she recovers. However, the fact that the humour ultimately "makes nothing happen" does not tell us why community-building laughter is so often associated with violence.

In order to begin to understand the association of this form of humour with violence, I would like to turn briefly to Clifford Geertz's important anthropological essay "Deep Play: Notes on the Balinese Cockfight." In his essay, Geertz analyzes the practice of cockfighting in Bali, a literal "contact sport." The fights are a "popular obsession" in Bali, participated in by the vast majority of the male populace, held in the town centres and associated symbolically with the men and with the island itself.[41]

Geertz identifies a number of seeming contradictions in this obsession. He notes that, despite their love of and identification with cockfighting, the Balinese are revolted by animality[42] and tend to be a subdued, cautious and controlled people who generally evade conflict.[43] There are parallels here to the use of humiliating or violent humour by North American Aboriginal people, who, like the Balinese, tend to value social harmony. Geertz also points out that cockfighting does not either increase or decrease the status of the men involved[44] nor does it tend to have a great economic impact.[45] In other words, like humour, cockfighting does not appear to actually "do" anything. So, Geertz wonders, why bother?

His proposed answer to this question resonates in interesting ways with the examples of humour raised in this essay. Geertz claims that the fights, precisely because they are set aside from life as "only a game," become symbolic moments in which the Balinese can articulate and perceive issues of status and hierarchy in their society. He explains that this articulation does not actually change anyone's status:

> What sets the cockfight apart from the ordinary course of life, lifts it from the realm of everyday practical affairs, and surrounds it with an aura of enlarged importance is not, as functionalist sociology would have it, that it reinforces status discriminations... but that it provides a metasocial commentary upon the whole matter of assorting human beings into fixed hierarchical ranks and thus organizing the major part of collective existence around that assortment. Its function, if you want to call it that, is interpretive.[46]

Because of their symbolic and interpretive functions, Geertz concludes, the Balinese cockfights must be read not as reflections of life in Bali but rather as texts that say something about that life, to be interpreted much as we would literary texts.[47]

In his essay, Geertz attempts to move anthropological method towards something resembling literary analysis. However, when it comes to Native literature, literary critics often move towards an anthropological mode, viewing the literature as a direct and transparent reflection of Native life. If we were to take such an ethnographic approach to humour, we would probably conclude that the violence in the humour in this chapter is simply a reflection of "problems"—violence, abuse, victimhood—in Native communities. But Geertz's comments suggest a less limited approach.

Humour, like cockfighting, is episodic, emotional and understood as somehow "lesser than" or detached from everyday life. As such, it becomes a way to displace, condense and examine various social tensions, anxieties and contradictions. Humour is an indirect means of thinking through contentious community issues. This view can help us to understand why Native writers, in depicting the use of humour within Native communities, would also depict a thread of violence. I would argue that humour allows the writers to reflect on and examine the process of community-building. As I have shown throughout, the depiction of people laughing together and teaching one another creates a warm sense of closeness, a sense of "Native community." However, the communitarian aim of complete social unity is impossible. There will always be an "outside" that does not easily fit within that community. The push towards unity may therefore cause the passive acceptance of violence (as with Nigger), the maintenance of self-destructive patterns (as with Aunty) or the violent push to control others (as with Jeremy and Tom). There is always an edge to community, an edge that lies between inclusion and exclusion, identification and alienation, power and victimhood, harmony and conflict. The Native writers I've drawn on in this essay use humour to face, examine and play with this edge. Hence humour is depicted not only as a moment of sharing but as a means of survival, a means of controlling others, or a means of expressing tense and morally complex situations.

"Community" has become something of a buzzword in discussions of Native literature. The word can be deceiving, since, as Raymond Williams points out, "Unlike all other terms of social organization (state, nation, society, etc.) it seems never to be used unfavourably and never to be given any positive opposing or distinguishing term."[48] Indeed, the use of "community" by critics of Aboriginal literature generally confirms Williams's suspicions—it is unexamined and given uniformly positive connotations. Native writers, however, while valuing and affirming Native community, critically examine the process of community building. This critical edge has been little noticed, perhaps because, as Robert Warrior argues, Native people have been acknowledged as producers of literature and culture but rarely as critics.[49] Warrior further points out that we can learn from the ability of Native creative writers to critically consider factors such as sovereignty, tradition and community without reducing them to absolutes.[50] Humour—with its basis in incongruity—offers these writers an effective way to maintain such a balance, both affirming and critiquing their communities.

— NOTES —

1. Greg Sarris, *Keeping Slug Woman Alive: A Holistic Approach to American Indian Texts*. Berkeley: University of California Press, 1993, p. 2.

2. Thomas King, in an interview with Hartmut Lutz. In *Contemporary Challenges: Conversations with Canadian Native Authors* by Hartmut Lutz. Saskatoon: Fifth House, 1991, p. 111.

3. Vine Deloria, *Custer Died for Your Sins: An Indian Manifesto*. New York: Macmillan, 1969, p. 169.

4. Clare Brant, "Native Ethics and Rules of Behaviour." *Canadian Journal of Psychiatry* 35-6 (1990), pp. 534–35.

5. Ibid., p. 535.

6. Fyre Jean Graveline, *Circle Works: Transforming Eurocentric Consciousness*. Halifax: Fernwood, 1998, p. 214.

7. Gerald Vizenor, quoted in *Roots of Survival: Native American Storytelling and the Sacred* by Joseph Bruchac. Golden, CO: Fulcrum, 1996, p. 309.

8. Catherine Fagan, personal communication, 2000.

9. Ian Ross, *fareWel*. Winnipeg: Scirocco Drama, 1997, p. 43.

10. Wilfred Pelletier, "Childhood in an Indian Village," *Two Articles*. Institute for Indian Studies, Rochdale College. Toronto: Neewin, 1970, p. 1.

11. Ross, p. 52.

12. Ibid., pp. 52–53.

13. Ruby Slipperjack, *Honour the Sun*. Winnipeg: Pemmican, 1987, p. 105.

14. Julie Cruikshank, *The Social Life of Stories: Narrative and Knowledge in the Yukon Territory*. Vancouver: UBC Press, 1998, pp. 340–41.

15. Slipperjack, p. 120.

16. Vi Hilbert, "Poking Fun in Lushootseed." In *Working Papers for the 18th International Conference on Salish and Neighboring Languages*. Seattle: University of Washington Press, 1983, p. 198.

17. Barre Toelken, "The 'Pretty Languages' of Yellowman: Genre, Mode, and Texture in Navaho Coyote Narratives." *Genre* 2 (1969), p. 228.

18. Laurence Millman, with John Poker, Tshinish Pasteen and Thomas Pastitshi, "How Wolverine Got Stuck in a Bear's Skull." In *Coming to Light: Contemporary Translations of the Native Literatures of North America*, ed. Brian Swann. New York: Vintage, 1994, p. 209.

19. Ibid., pp. 218–19.

20. Gregory Scofield, *I Knew Two Metis Women*. Victoria: Polestar, 1999, p. 30.

21. Ibid., p. 53.

22. Ibid., p. 50.

23. Ibid., p. 51.

24. Louise Halfe, *Bear Bones & Feathers*. Regina: Coteau, 1994, pp. 39–40.

25. Ibid., p. 30.

26. Ibid., p. 32.

27. Tomson Highway, *Kiss of the Fur Queen*. Toronto: Doubleday Canada, 1998, p. 233.

28. Joseph Bruchac, *Roots of Survival: Native American Storytelling and the Sacred*. Golden, CO: Fulcrum, 1996, p. 159.

29. Vine Deloria, *Custer Died for Your Sins: An Indian Manifesto*. New York: Macmillan, 1969, p. 263.

30. Jean-Guy A. Goulet, *Ways of Knowing: Experience, Knowledge, and Power Among the Dene Tha*. Lincoln and London: University of Nebraska Press, 1998, pp. 185–86.

31. Marilyn Dumont, "Fireflies," *A Really Good Brown Girl*. London, ON: Brick, 1996, p. 69.

32. Ibid., p. 69.

33. Slipperjack, p. 82.

34. Ibid., p. 86.

35. Ibid., p. 86.

36. Ibid., p. 86.

37. James F. English, *Comic Transactions: Literature, Humor, and the Politics of Community in Twentieth-Century Britain*. Ithaca and London: Cornell University Press, 1994, p. 28.

38. Eden Robinson, "Contact Sports," *Traplines*. New York: Metropolitan, 1996, p. 91.

39. Ibid., p. 93.

40. Ibid., p. 101.

41. Clifford Geertz, "Deep Play: Notes on the Balinese Cockfight." *Daedalus* 101 (1972), pp. 5–8.

42. Ibid., pp. 6–7.

43. Ibid., p. 25.

44. Ibid., p. 23.

45. Ibid., pp. 16–17.

46. Ibid., p. 26.

47. Ibid., p. 26.

48. Raymond Williams, *Keywords: A Vocabulary of Culture and Society*, rev. ed. Glasgow: Fontana, 1979, p. 66.

49. Robert Warrior, *Tribal Secrets: Recovering American Indian Intellectual Traditions*. Minneapolis: University of Minnesota Press, 1994, p. xvi.

50. Ibid., p. 118.

*Astutely* selected **ETHNO-BASED**
examples of **CULTURAL** *jocularity* and
*racial* **COMICALNESS**

. . . . . . . .

{ **EXAMPLE 1** }

A YOUNG, WHITE *city boy decided that there might be a good business in supplying remote communities by plane. He decided to first go out into some of these areas and get to know a few key people to judge their needs. So he flew to one community and asked the man at the airstrip, If a white man was to talk to only one person in the community, who should that be? The man at the airstrip answered, "Oh, that's an easy one. You have to talk to Old Nanabush. He's absolutely amazing. He knows everybody and he knows everything. Everything! He never forgets anything. He's got a steel-trap mind."*

*Well, the young businessman was intrigued. So he went off to meet the old man and test him. He wasn't too sure that the guy at the airstrip hadn't been pulling his leg. But after talking to Nanabush, the white guy was pretty impressed. Nanabush really did seem to know everything. So the young man said, "The guy at the airstrip said you never forget anything. What did you have for breakfast on January 12, two years ago?"*

*The old man said, "Well, that was a Tuesday, and I had a little bannock, and I remember Geeshick had gone ice fishing the day before, so I had me some good fried fish too. And two eggs, I believe." Of course the businessman realized that Nanabush could be making it all up to have some fun with the city kid, so he politely thanked Nanabush for his time and went on his way.*

A few years into his operation, the businessman decided to once again visit the communities along his supply route. Of course he had to go see Nanabush and, perhaps, have a little fun with the old man. So he walked through the village and met Nanabush again, who was sitting on his porch, just like he had been a few years back. The businessman walked over, raised his hand in a sign of hello and said the standard Indian greeting, "How."

Nanabush looked up from his chair and said, "Scrambled."

{ EXAMPLE 2 }

THERE WAS A *Ministry of Natural Resources officer who heard a rumour of a Native man fishing illegally. The officer went to the pier and spotted an older Native man getting ready to go out on the water. The MNR officer asked the man if he could go fishing with him. The Native man looked at the officer and said, "Sure, get in."*

*The officer and the Native man motored to the middle of the bay, where the Native man opened up his tackle box and pulled out a stick of dynamite. The officer couldn't believe his eyes when the dynamite was lit and thrown into the water. As the dynamite exploded, fish started appearing on the surface of the water. The officer jumped up and yelled at the Native man, "Do you know that I can confiscate everything you own and give you a huge fine and jail time for that?"*

*The Native man reached into the tackle box, lit another stick of dynamite, gave it to the officer and said, "Are you going to fish or are you going to talk?"*

{ EXAMPLE 3 }

SO, THESE THREE *Aboriginal women all died at the same time, and they found themselves standing together at the gate to Heaven. St. Peter was there, sitting in judgement in his big celestial chair. Now, St. Peter usually sent Aboriginal people to Hell without so much as a hearing, but he was intrigued by the fact of these three women all dying at the same time. So he thought he'd give them a break and at least see if they were good people.*

*The first woman he turned to was Lakota. "Well," said St. Peter, "I usually just send all you pagans to Hell, but if you can make a good accounting of your life, I might just let you in." So the Lakota woman says, "Well, you know, the White Buffalo Calf Woman came to us and gave us the Pipe and instructions on its use and on how to lead a good life. So that's the way that I followed." St. Peter said, "Well, that sounds like a pretty good way of life. I will let you into Heaven."*

*The second woman was Ojibway, and St. Peter asked her the same question: "Would you care to account for your life?" The Ojibway woman answered that she was a follower of the Midewiwin tradition. It had been given to the Ojibway so long ago that they couldn't remember when, but they believed that the Creator wanted them to live their lives in that way. "And so I did!" the Ojibway woman said. St. Peter was touched by her sincerity, so he let her into Heaven as well.*

*The third woman was Mohawk. St. Peter turned to her and asked if she had anything she wanted to say to him. Without a pause, the Mohawk woman said, "Would you mind getting up? You're sitting in my chair!"*

# AND NOW, LADIES AND GENTLEMEN,

......................................

*Get* READY *for Some*
*(Ab)*ORIGINAL *Stand-up* COMEDY

.............

{ DON KELLY }

*(Polite applause)*

**T**HANKS, FOLKS. *My name is Don Kelly, and I'm a Native-Canadian, Ojibway Indian. There aren't a lot of us doing stand-up comedy. In fact, my agent keeps telling me I should play it up more, maybe use my Indian name as my stage name. But I'm going to stick with Don Kelly, because my Indian name is Runs-Like-a-Girl.*

It's been said that simply being born Native in Canada is a political act. You're a walking shadow of the unfinished business that hangs over the country, an uncomfortable reminder of the reality that gives lie to Canada's cherished self-image as a fair and just country. You're Canada's living, breathing, dirty little secret.

In other words, a prime topic for feel-good comedy! The jokes just write themselves.

*Thanks for that laughter, folks. I'll pass your positive response on to my agent, Bouncing Cheque!*

It's easier to get your foot in the door wearing a silly grin instead of a scowl. Why kick the door down when you can get them to invite you in? "Runs-Like-a-Girl," silly as it is, opens the door. And once the door is open, then you can start hauling in the baggage.

*People ask me how an Ojibway Indian ended up with the name "Kelly." This goes back about a hundred years, to when the government wanted to pen us up on reserves. They'd send some lackey around to get everyone's name so they could make a "band list." So, typically, some English guy would go up to my great-great-great grandfather:*

*"And your name is, sir?"*

*"Paybahnahgahbow Shonya Gwaneb Dezhnkhaz Onigaming Danjobah Pizhew nTotem."*

*(Pause)*

*"Okay...Mr. Kelly! Yeah, we're spelling it 'Kelly.' You can pronounce it any way you want. Knock yourself out!"*

Tension can be good for stand-up comedy. A stand-up act is often a cycle of tension and release, tension and release.

Sometimes I can feel a crowd stiffen up the second I mention I'm Native Canadian. "Ooh—are we going to get harangued about the evils of white society and the injustices perpetrated against Native people? Is this going to be an hour of guilt and shame?" Or I can feel another kind of tension: the uncomfortable anticipation of an hour of racial slurs. "Ooh—is he going to confront us with every negative stereotype we've ever heard? Is it going to be an hour of shock comedy? Is he going to drag that drunk, lazy Indian stereotype out on stage and throw him into the spotlight?" I mean, if Native issues are a touchy topic in living rooms and chat rooms across the country, then why should comedy clubs be any different?

*I hope I'm not offending anyone, folks. If I have, well, as we Indians say: Boy, is my face red!*

I've been doing stand-up comedy at clubs and conferences, roadhouses and festivals for almost a decade now. (You say you've never heard of me? Welcome to Canadian showbiz!) I've been a fan of stand-up comedy since I was a young brave. I always knew I wanted to try it one day.

Admittedly, stand-up comedy is a weird thing for anyone to aspire to, Native or otherwise. It's definitely not for everyone. Notice how whenever they survey people on their biggest fears the top two are always (a) public speaking and (b) dying. Stand-up comedy has a wonderful way of combining the two into one big knot of anxiety.

Still, I knew I had to do it. And I knew that when I did I'd work on material about Native people and the "Indian experience" in Canada.

For one thing, I'd never heard that topic discussed on a comedy stage. Sure, Charlie Hill, an Oneida from Wisconsin, was working U.S. clubs way back in the early 1970s. He was by most accounts the first. (And when you're Indian, it's all about being first.) He wrote pretty much all the lines that have become quotable classics for us Native folk. "Take my land—please!" Or greeting the crowd with a rhythmic powwow chant: "Hey-How-Are-Ya-Hey-How-Are-Ya..."

But Native stand-up comedy is still a newcomer to the stage. We're still writing our own creation stories. And it's great to be in on the ground level in undiscovered country. There's so much new territory to explore.

*I'm an Aboriginal citizen living in Canada. And I just want to say to you, on behalf of all of us: We love what you've done with the place.*

These days there are a handful of Native comics in Canada. Of those, few are doing the mainstream comedy-club circuit. Two guys I cross paths with are Howie Miller, who's based in Edmonton, Alberta, and Gerry "the Big Bear" Barrett, who works out of Winnipeg, Manitoba. There may be others I haven't heard of, but I *can* say that the market is far from saturated.

There's another group of performers who mainly stick to the conference circuit or special "Aboriginal" shows. One of the best-known Native comedians, Don Burnstick, a Cree from Alexander First Nation in Alberta, is big on this circuit. He doesn't even play the clubs. For Don, who is upfront about his past battles with substance abuse, it's a personal decision to pursue the wellness and healing path and avoid venues where the alcohol is as much of a draw as the entertainment. For others, conferences and theatre shows are the more comfortable and reliable gigs, because there's a built-in audience ready and willing to hear all about the Native experience. Clubs and road gigs are a little dicier. The audiences are coming for laughs and beer (lots and lots of beer). They're not seeking enlightenment or epiphanies—they want escape. They want to put their brains in neutral and let someone else drive the bus.

They're coming to comedy clubs for a lot of reasons. But a dissection of race relations in Canada is probably not one of them.

*Native people are the Rodney Dangerfield of Canadian society— we get no respect. I mean, we're the only people where it's okay to name vehicles after us. Vehicles!*

*"Hey, Don, check out that Pontiac and that Winnebago. What do you think of that Jeep Cherokee?"*

*"Well, I kinda like that Ford Negro myself. And that Dodge Quadriplegic."*

*Is this okay for anyone else?*

Native comedy can be touchy for non-Aboriginal people. In these days of political correctness, even the pure of heart and well-intentioned can find it conflicting.

"If I laugh at that joke am I laughing at Native people? If I laugh at that stereotype am I admitting that it's true? If I don't laugh am I offending the poor Indian on stage? If he's making fun of himself, can I laugh? Or should I take the high road and…" At this point said individual's head usually explodes, which distracts from the show and forces me to end my set early.

But seriously… I'm aware of this tension. Early on I had to experiment with different ways of getting the audience to relax so they could listen, laugh and enjoy the ride. When I'm about to take my passengers on a delightful sightseeing trip through the minefield of race relations in Canada, I try to ease them into the drive. So I start with "Runs-Like-a-Girl." (Hope the ladies aren't offended!) It sends up a smoke signal that says this isn't going to be a heavy lecture. I can laugh at myself. And we can laugh together, and at one another.

That's more my style anyway. I'm not in-your-face (or in-your-anything, for that matter). My comedy style is not that of the pit bull. I'm more of a golden retriever—you know, friendly, well-groomed, and I drool a lot when excited.

Still, I also have to deal with the surprised response I often get when people find out that I'm First Nations. How can I put this?

*People tell me I don't look Native. I believe the politically correct term is "pigmentally challenged." I am "melanin deprived."*

*That's why I don't use the term "white people." I know the second I do, you'll be like: "Uh, have you looked in a mirror lately, Casper?"*

If the revolution ever hits, I'll make a great Stealth Indian.

The "pigmentally challenged" bit is not always a killer, but sometimes it's necessary. Audiences don't always believe I'm Ojibway, and the last thing I want is for them to think I'm faking it for the material. (The DNA equivalent of a prop act—for shame!)

There's an old rule in stand-up comedy that you need to address immediately anything that's obvious about yourself. If you're really fat, talk about it right off the top. If you're really tall, talk about it right off the top. If you're a dwarf in an iron lung... maybe stand-up's not for you. But if you do it, talk about it right off the top. Because that's what the audience is looking at and thinking about. If you don't deal with it you're running uphill. It's distracting from your material. They're too busy marvelling at how tall/fat/elfin you are to listen to your pithy observations about airplane food and television commercials.

So for me, it's a little trickier. I let them know I'm Native Canadian, then I have to deal with the obvious: that I don't look Native. When I did the TV talk show *Open Mike with Mike Bullard* a few years back, Bullard leaned over to me and said: "I can't think of anything worse than being an Indian who looks like Custer."

*Like most things in my life, I blame it on Mom. Dad is full Ojibway, all the way back. But Mom has no Native blood. In fact, she's Swedish. So she's not just white—she's downright pale.*

*And I know you're all thinking of your own little joke for that: "Ojibway and Swedish? So how's it going there, 'Dances-with-Bjorn'? I'm sure you have the marvellous ability to track game while assembling Ikea furniture!"*

Who knows—the "look" thing may even do some good in a small way. Maybe it challenges the audience's preconceived notions about Native people. Maybe they'll realize that not all First Nations people fit their frame of reference. First of all, there's my physical look. No leathers, feathers, braids or beads.

Second, they see me in an environment where we're all laughing. How often do they see Indians in that kind of situation? A lot of Canadians see us only in formal settings (a lecture or conference) or, shall we say, less formal situations (stumbling down Main Street). Or on the evening news, with some irate Indian politician reciting a litany of lamentations.

It's good to break the mould. It expands people's ideas about what and who and where and how is an Indian. A little public education helps. And it's sorely needed in this country.

*I saw in the news that the leader of the Conservative Party of Canada sent a congratulatory letter to all the Indian Friendship Centres in the country, wishing them a "Happy Republic of India Day." India? Come on. Granted, Columbus made the same mistake, but that was five hundred years ago!*

*He blames it on a clerical error. They searched their mailing list for anything with "India" or "Indian" in the title and it spat out all those names. I'll give him the benefit of the doubt, but I can hardly wait until Gay Pride Week when he sends that wonderful letter to the Lebanese community.*

The best thing about comedy—and the best thing about being a Native comic—is that you get to sneak in some points, maybe even make a statement or two.

I can't claim that my act is heavy on the profundities. Fact is, I enjoy being silly. I try to craft material that's sharp and clever, but that doesn't mean it's all politics and punditry. There's a balance.

It's true that in stand-up, anything goes. It's one of the last bastions of free speech. Some take that as a licence to shock, to whack patrons over the head with a two-by-four labelled TABOO and with a bloody nail poking out the end. I won't dismiss that out of hand, though. Shock and awe can get a reaction. Sometimes a violent one, sometimes a laugh. But if it's pure shock value with no substance, it's kind of cheesy. Now, it's fun to be cheesy—we all need a little cheese in our diet. But we also need some fibre, something with more substance to chew on for nourishment.

Freedom, to me, entails responsibility—the responsibility to handle a topic in an appropriate manner. A great, wise man once said: "With great power comes great responsibility." (I believe it was Spider-man.) The way I see it—and this is just me talkin'!—comedians get the distinct privilege of having a captive and (ideally) attentive audience listening for ten, fifteen, thirty, forty-five or however many minutes. Why not try to sneak in an idea or two?

*I was doing this gig up in a small town in northern Ontario. Yeah, I was up there doing the big Just for Nothing Festival. But I got asked one of the best questions I've ever heard.*

*This woman comes up after the show and says: "Hey, Native Guy, I've always wondered something about your people: Do your people celebrate Thanksgiving?"*

*How can I resist that?*

*"Yeah! Just last year I had a traditional Native Thanksgiving. The European guy who lives next door came over, claimed he 'discovered' my apartment and now he's living in the place!"*

That's one of my favourite bits. Fine, maybe it's not Mort Sahl. But it makes a point. I get to use my apartment as a microcosm of the world, and in doing so shatter the entire myth of "discovery" and *terra nullius*. (*Terra nullius*: Latin for "inconveniently populated.") When people laugh that means they get it. Not just the joke—they get the point. If they didn't get the connection they wouldn't be laughing. I'm happy to say they usually do laugh. And maybe, just maybe, one person thinks a little bit about it.

Humour is a fantastic communications device. If you yell at people or browbeat them into submission, they'll tune out and walk away. But if you can keep them laughing, they'll keep listening. People who would never walk into a lecture on Native history will walk into a comedy club. And someone who walks into a lecture on First Nations history is probably halfway sold anyway. We need to start preaching to the pagans. Do a little converting of our own. Get in their face, Jesuit-style.

*"Oh sure, my neighbour kept a little spot in 'reserve' for me. It's right next to the cat's litter box—thanks a lot! I'm not sure how I'm gonna get my apartment back, but I'm thinking of blockading the bathroom. That's one stand-off I'm pretty sure I can win."*

I said earlier I'm not an aggressive comic. But they are out there. The aforementioned Howie Miller is most definitely in-your-face, likeable though he is. Howie'll deal with stereotypes and racial slurs head-on, no mercy and no apologies. Any audience members who challenge him do so at their own risk.

It's interesting to me that there aren't more angry Native comics. We have a lot to be angry about. I've tried to write angry material, but it just doesn't jibe with my style or persona, on stage or off. I'm reminded of the cautionary tale of Dick Gregory, a brilliant black American comic who was active in the comedy scene and the civil rights movement in the 1960s. He eventually gave up comedy because, as he famously said, "After a while, it's just not funny any more."

Personally, I love comedians who can mine the most toxic topics for relevant insights and social satire. Words carry a lot of weight. And when they're burdened with the extra baggage of race and politics, they can be too heavy for some people to carry.

*The term that bothers me the most is "Indian giver." Hey—we were the ones who got all the promises from you guys. "Share the land and we'll give you this. Sign this treaty and we'll give you that." And then you don't deliver. And we get tagged with this term "Indian giver"? Come on—that's like saying to your black boss, "What are you—some kind of slave driver?" The irony's a little thick, people.*

Race and stereotypes. Tricky topics. And there are two ways to get laughs about them: by refuting them or by reinforcing them.

It's parallel to the kinds of laughs you can get in comedy in general. First, there's the laughter that comes from crystallizing an idea the audience already knows. It's the laughter of recognition. (For example, the familiar joke of telling an American, "Watch out for Canadian beer—it's got alcohol in it!")

Then there's the laughter of "the new"—communicating an original idea or making connections between things that the audience didn't know were there. Jerry Seinfeld is a master of this. (Take for example his bit about laundry night being like a party for your clothes.) Seinfeld mines comedy from the utterly mundane things that we all look at every day. He takes a topic and peers underneath it, turns it over and looks at it from different angles. I mean, the guy had a five-minute bit about cotton balls. A hilarious bit... about cotton balls. Write me one hilarious joke about cotton balls and I'll buy it. (I've got some nice shiny trinkets...)

That same dynamic ("the recognized" vs. "the new") applies to jokes about stereotypes. It's easier to get laughs by reinforcing stereotypes. You can rely on the audience's mental shorthand to make the connection. But to be honest, it's a cheaper laugh.

Now, I'm not getting all holier than thou. (What's the Ojibway equivalent of "holier than thou"? Perhaps, in recognition of our sweat lodge ceremony, it's "sweatier than thou"?) I admit I have material that reinforces the stereotype.

*I was trying to be cool with my girlfriend at the reserve by talking that sexy dirty talk. Turns out it doesn't really go over well on the rez.*

*I'm like: "Who's your daddy! Who's your daddy!"*

*And she says: "I don't know…"*

*Really killed the mood.*

So, guilty as charged. But I'd rather accentuate the positive than reinforce the negative. My rationale is this: If I get a laugh by reinforcing a stereotype I'm basically saying that the stereotype is true. That's not too harmful when it's about bingo. It's more problematic when it's about alcoholism or welfare. If I do jokes that reinforce stereotypes then all I'm doing is telling the redneck in the crowd that he's right. He can run out into the street and repeat my joke, and if anyone calls him on it he can say: "Well, the Indian at the comedy club said it, why can't I?" And he's got a point. So I'd rather play with the stereotype than play up the stereotype.

*So I'm half Native and half white. It's an interesting dichotomy. I often find my white side tries to exploit my Native side. It's true. I'll give you a real-life example: Let's say I walk into a bank and there's a huge mob, a massive crush of people waiting to be served. The teller will come out and say: "Okay, who was here first?" and I'll go, "Well, technically, moi. I don't want to start a Supreme Court case about it… but I will." Because face it, gang, I've got you either way. Dad is Ojibway, that's First Nations. Mom is Swedish, which is basically Viking. So either way, dibs on the land!*

So what is Native humour? Let's step back to look at the beast.

I'll start by making the obvious point that there are as many kinds of Native comedy as there are Native comics. (So in Canada that would mean seven—kidding!) But I think we can point to a couple of common characteristics.

First, it's all about the teasing. Don Burnstick uses the example of two white guys walking together. When one of them slips and falls, the other one rushes over to help him, frantically asking: "Are you okay? Are you all right? Let me help you up."

Meanwhile, across the street, two Native guys are walking. One of them slips and falls. The other guy laughs hysterically, then rushes over and helps the first guy up. The first guy probably contemplates a lawsuit, because odds are, if there are two or more Indians together, one of them's a lawyer.

Fact is, we can laugh at ourselves better than anyone else can. Some of the best (and worst) Indian jokes I've ever heard were told to me by Indians.

The other characteristic of Native humour is a tendency towards self-deprecation. A lot of Native humour is about taking ourselves down a peg. The joke's on me. In one way, this is just the other side of the teasing coin—teasing turned inwards.

Now, we can stretch a bit and make a cultural connection by tying teasing and self-deprecation to our Trickster legends. (As this is an article on Native humour, I am legally obligated to make a Trickster reference.) In our Ojibway Trickster stories, we call him Nanaboozhoo. Nanaboozhoo is a powerful spirit, but he is not Christ-like. Nanaboozhoo would have tripped as he made his way up Calvary or done a first-class spit-take after John baptized him. Nanaboozhoo is a mischievous, sometimes foolish spirit, but always creative.

What I remember about our Trickster stories is that Nanaboozhoo always plays games with people that make them look silly, that embarrass them. And, in turn, the minute he starts feeling a little too proud, he'll slip and fall into the dung heap. He is more Jack Tripper than Jesus, come to think of it. The message in many of these stories is, basically, don't get too full of yourself. Don't take yourself too seriously. There's only so much we can control, and the rest is nature.

The other notable thing about our stories is that they're built on the oral tradition. Telling them is half the fun. The outline is constant, but the teller can stretch the story, change the emphasis or revise it based on the audience reaction. Our storytellers were working the room long before there were comedy clubs.

*I had a rough childhood. Very traumatic. My father drove a wood-panelled station wagon. Yep, it was tough. We'd have to pile in in broad daylight and actually be seen cruising around in a wood-panelled station wagon. I just took comfort in the fact that we're an Ojibway family. I figured anyone who saw us would assume we had made it ourselves.*

*"Look, Junior! There goes a traditional Ojibway family in one of those birchbark sedans they build so well. You know, they use them when they hunt moose so they blend in with their surroundings."*

And what about recent history? Some would argue that Native humour is part of a tradition we could call "the comedy of coping"—humour as a response to troubling times, dark days and oppression. People often apply this same theory to Jewish comedy.

But to me, the two arguments cancel each other out. Can we really have it both ways? Either we've always had humour and laughter pumping through the veins of our culture (witness the legends and stories), or we developed humour as a reaction to a history of being dispossessed, disenfranchised, discounted and dismissed. I believe that humour has always been there, in ourselves and in our culture. Perhaps the last couple of centuries have sharpened and honed our wit, but laughter has echoed across Turtle Island for centuries.

*As an oppressed minority, I like getting together with other oppressed minorities to play our traditional games. My personal favourite is "Pin the Blame on the Honky."*

Regardless of where our humour comes from, I'm glad to be part of a vital and growing community of Native comics. It's energizing to see such a range of talent. I've never wanted to be a "Native comic" per se. I've always wanted to be a comic—a comic who's Native, certainly, and who talks about it, but one who talks about a lot of other things too. It could be because I grew up mainly in the city. I had other friends and influences. I don't see everything I do through the lens of "First Nations citizen." Like, when I order a pizza, I don't obsess for hours about how I, as a Native Canadian, feel about picking up the phone and ordering this pizza. (Although I do feel guilty if I order the buffalo wings. Typical white people—hunt the buffalo and take only the wings.)

But I have no problem with First Nations comics who want to be, first and foremost, First Nations comics—more power to them. In fact, we need them. We need the full range because we are diverse peoples.

*We need more Native comedians and more Native performers. It's a dream of mine to one day see a Native actor playing Hamlet, that most classic of traditional English theatre roles.*

*I could just imagine a Native actor playing Hamlet, delivering that dramatic soliloquy: "To be, or not to be. Under the B...2."*

March 24, 2004, was a landmark day for Native comedy in Canada.

On that day, the CBC Winnipeg Comedy Festival presented a special show called the Turtle Island Gala. It was the first time to my knowledge that any festival has presented a show consisting entirely of Aboriginal comedians. Everyone was there: Don Burnstick, Howie Miller, Gerry Barrett—they even brought in Charlie Hill from the United States. I had the great honour to be part of it.

It was a tremendous mix of acts, and a tremendous night. The crowd loved it. And I am proud to say that the crowd got a first-class comedy show, not a first-class Native comedy show. The Turtle Island Gala held its own with the other shows at the festival. It was a welcome recognition that we have the talent in Indian country to put on a first-class gala. It was proof that we can present a show that entertains everyone, not just our own people. Laughter is universal.

Comedy is well-trod ground, but Native stand-up comedy is wide-open terrain. There are no boundaries and no borders. It's undiscovered country. And our people are experts in navigating new territory. Why not explore and see what you find? Who knows—you may even find yourself. Or at least find yourself laughing.

*Well, you've been great, but I should really get going, folks. I'd love to stick around longer but, hey—land don't claim itself!*
   *Good night.*

# WHACKING THE INDIGENOUS FUNNY BONE

*Political* CORRECTNESS
*vs.* NATIVE *Humour, Round* ONE

{ DREW HAYDEN TAYLOR }

Humour is widely used by Indians to deal with life.
Indian gatherings are marked by laughter and jokes, many
directed at the horrors of history, and at the continuing
impact of colonization, and at the biting knowledge that
living as an exile in one's own land necessitates.

PAULA GUNN ALLEN

Tribal [humour] tends to be "inside" and might be
viewed as sexist, racist and all that... but is really designed
to keep folks with ample reason to do so from going off
the deep end; hence it is in its way anti-racist.

WARD CHURCHILL[1]

𝒩OT LONG ago, I was speaking at a high school in Ottawa, one that focussed on the arts. I was there to chat about being a professional Native playwright/writer/humorist because several of the students had read and studied my material. Overall, my talk went well, and I was deep into the question-and-answer section of my presentation when, at the prodding of a teacher, a young Caucasian teenager put up his hand. He didn't know exactly how to phrase his question, and there was substantial hemming and hawing, but in the end he managed to articulate something that had been bothering him.

"How can you get away writing what you do about white people?"

A fair enough question. In my writing, I often poke fun at the dominant culture, in what I believe to be a kind-hearted, inoffensive way, as any satirist might. As one example, I've come up with alternative names for people of the Caucasian race: people of pallor, pigment-denied, colour-challenged and melanin-deprived, to name just a few. Evidently the teenager, as a member of this community, felt that my comments were politically incorrect and wondered why there hadn't been more of an outcry about them.

A few years earlier a similar concern had been expressed in Vancouver, albeit in a much more dramatic fashion. A production of my play *alternatives,* a sort of intellectual satire, received a bomb threat; somebody phoned in to say, "If this theatre continues to produce plays that are racist against white people, don't be surprised at what we leave behind." Luckily the bomb squad didn't find anything, though I'm sure a few plays have bombed, rather than been bombed, at that theatre. *alternatives* takes place at a dinner party. It pokes fun at Native/non-Native relationships, with one of the more contentious (I say that sarcastically) and explosive (no pun intended) jokes occurring when one of the white guests gets angry and says she's going home. To which a Native guest replies, "Home? To Europe?"

After spending fifteen years writing humour, researching the topic and visiting more than 120 Native communities (not including those in urban environments), it's my observation that Native humour often crosses the tenuous and ambiguous boundary between the politically correct and the politically incorrect. Native humour pushes the envelope. It asks questions. It makes statements. It goes places polite and civil humour won't go. It reflects injustice and anger. It showcases observation and commentary. And it's located somewhere between the heart, the belly and the crotch. Although it may not be politically correct to say so, I do think it's possible to have a Native sense of humour without being Native, just like a Native person can have a Mercedes-Benz (complete with authorized ownership papers and everything!) without being white. But both these things are rare.

Native humour comes from five hundred years of colonization, of oppression, of being kept prisoners in our own country. With legalized attacks on our culture, our languages, our identities and even our religion, often the only way left for Native people to respond to the cruel realities of Fourth World existence was in humour. Humour kept us sane. It gave us power. It gave us privacy. Whenever two First Nations people got together, something magical was sure to happen: there would be laughter. Whether it was children in a residential school, or people on the trapline, or a bunch of guys working high steel, Native humour was a little bit of home tucked away for when we needed it. Sort of like spiritual pemmican.

A good portion of Native humour springs from a sense of survival. Frequently, it's a reaction against the world. And anything born of survival will have barbs and sharp teeth attached, to provide protection and refuge. Humour can also take the bruises and scars of depression, oppression and suppression and act as a salve or tonic to take the pain away. It often works as an antidote, even. As I once heard an elder from the Blood Reserve say,

"Humour is the WD-40 of healing." So Native humour is multi-purposed: it can cause pain as well as heal it.

But not all Native humour is aggressive. A large portion of it comes from the desire to share good times and happy thoughts and the need to deal with the absurdities of everyday life. For people travelling on the trapline, living in tepees or spending days out fishing, the only entertainment available was humour, whether in jokes or in storytelling. Stories that could make people laugh were respected indeed. Humour and storytelling are kissing cousins.

Over the years, the concept of political correctness has developed into a double-edged sword. Originally seen as a way of instituting equality and respect among people of different races, economic groups, genders and religious backgrounds, it has evolved into a rigid construct with specific boundaries and rules. Some people argue that in its attempts to liberate, political correctness has created restraints. Accusing someone of being "politically incorrect" means they are inconsiderate, rude, insensitive, brutish and anti-social. This is usually because they have made a comment or joke at the expense of a person different from themselves.

Introducing the First Nations identity into this environment, or the identity of any other oppressed, marginalized population, sets the normal perspective of what is allowed a little off centre. Humour, by its nature, is often at somebody's expense. Rare is the joke that has no victim. That immediately makes it a potentially "oppressive" medium.

*"What do you call a politically correct comic? Boring."*

Add to that volatile mixture the teasing and survival humour common in First Nations humour, and conflict with political correctness is bound to happen.

As any first-year academic will tell you, nothing is real or can be studied until it's been deconstructed. So let's do that with political correctness. We can begin by picturing a graph with an x-axis and a y-axis. On the x-axis are people from marginalized backgrounds, with the most oppressed or suppressed at the bottom, gradually working their way up the "socially accepted" ladder—let's call it the Ladder of Status—to the top. The list includes "niggers," "kikes," "chinks," "fags," "dykes," "dagos," "micks," "chicks," etc., on up to the top, where the male honky proudly surveys the graph, no doubt complimenting himself on discovering and culturally appropriating it. Part of the fun of this graph is trying to figure out the rankings—who is more oppressed on the Oppress-o-meter.

On the y-axis are jokes dealing with race, ethnicity, religion or some other aspect of culture. Now the fun begins, working from the bottom up. That is to say, on this social ladder, those situated at the top cannot make jokes aimed at those towards the bottom. In this instance, being part of the privileged elite is a limitation. Successful jokes are filled with helium, not lead. Those at the bottom, however, can make those higher up the social ladder the butt of their jokes. Witness the comedic material of African-American, Asian or Native comedians. A large part of their act often consists of making fun of the dominant white culture. It should also be acknowledged that humour can work sideways. Native people can make fun of each other and of anyone who is better off than they are, or who has the same approximate position on the Ladder of Status.

For instance, take a joke like:

> "How many Indians does it take to eat a rabbit? Two—one to eat it, the other to watch for cars."

If a non-Native person told that joke, there would be some serious scalping in store. Yet that joke was told to me by Thomas

King, the well-known Native humorist and author. I recipro-
cated by telling him one:

> "How can you get twenty-four Indians into the back of a Volks-
> wagen Bug? Simple: throw a case of beer on the back seat."

A mutual friend of ours, a Cherokee university professor from
the States, added to the mix:

> "What do you call a seven-course dinner in Lakota country?
> One dog and a six pack."

Natives and alcohol, a testy subject. Not one you're usually
expecting a joke about. And again, not a joke a white person
could tell. But I can, courtesy of my status card (which, ironically, is closely linked to the previously mentioned Ladder of
Status).

As described, the Ladder of Status allows some lateral
movement. I once attended a party with several noted Indo-
Canadians. I was there with another Native person. As often
happens at parties, we all started telling stories and jokes and
it wasn't long before the confusion began regarding the term
"Indian." So before you knew it, people were starting their stories
with "There was this Indian guy, a dot Indian" (putting a finger
to our foreheads), "not a feather Indian" (sticking two fingers
up behind our heads to indicate the feathers frequently seen on
pseudo-Native headbands). There were peals of laughter from
everyone in the room, and nobody felt insulted.

There are some exceptions to the Ladder of Status rules. I
have seen many white comedians (as well as black ones) make
fun of the lack of rhythm or dancing ability inherent in the Caucasian race and how supreme this ability is in the black community. But you will notice a joke like that is not a criticism but a
"compliment" to African-Americans. Same with the innumerable
penis-size jokes. Because these are supposedly complimentary,

they are excused from the "politically incorrect" rule. Sometimes, though, a "compliment" can go over the top—for example, a joke from a white comic about Asians having the natural ability to understand and deal with anything electronic. It does get complicated.

Now let's go back to our graph. On its flip side is a pyramid. Like the graph, the pyramid illustrates social status in North America. But the pyramid represents the theory that racism works only from the top down—racism is filled with lead, not helium. Only those at the top, the few in a place of privilege, are able to be racist. For instance, white people can be racist against Native, Asian or black people, but it is not technically possible for a black person to be racist against a white person. Wrong direction. The pyramid also works for sexism. A man can be sexist, but it's difficult for a woman to be. It all boils down to power, or the lack of it. (I'm not sure I *completely* agree with the hypothesis this pyramid presents, but I'll save that discussion for another day.)

The argument over the political correctness of Native humour can also be explored via the more common discussion revolving around the concept of cultural appropriation. This is an issue that has befuddled and angered both the Native and the non-Native arts communities for years. Should non-Natives write, create or tell anything Native? A simple enough question, with a not-so-simple answer.

To my way of thinking, it all has to do with spheres of knowledge. Consider it Aboriginal geometry. Within your sphere of knowledge is your life. Everything you have learned, everything you have experienced, everything you have participated in, everything you have come to understand lies within your sphere. Everybody has one. Some things in it are positive, some negative. In relation to cultural appropriation, it can be argued that you should write only about something within your own sphere of knowledge. Otherwise, you're intruding on another person's (or culture's) sphere. Once outside your personal sphere of knowledge, you are in danger of ramming into another sphere, potentially causing great damage to both spheres—and I'm not sure what the deductible is on spheres of knowledge.

The same principle can be applied to the world of politically correct humour. When you're making a joke, it is prudent to ensure the subject you're making fun of lies within your sphere of knowledge. If not, then it becomes politically incorrect. For example, if you're a white person, it is logical to make fun of white people. Venturing outside that sphere of knowledge can reveal your ignorance and affect the nature of your humour. What does a white person know about life on the reserve or in a poor black neighbourhood? Yet there are exceptions. When people take the time to acquire additional knowledge, to do their research—yes, even white people—then their spheres of knowledge grow. I have come across many non-Native people who have either lived in Native communities or worked extensively on an equal basis with Native people. Their spheres of knowledge can encompass the Native community. So it is possible, in some circumstances, for a white person to tell a Native joke without the charge of political incorrectness being thrown at him or her. Admittedly, the very colour of their skin places them in a more advantageous position on the Ladder of Status, but if they have put in their time and done their fieldwork on the same rung as Aboriginal people, a special visa can be issued. Nevertheless, it is a purely subjective situation. Each sphere of knowledge has definite boundaries, and woe betide those who cross those borders uninvited.

Native humour has two primary characteristics. That's saying a lot, considering that there are over six hundred Native communities across Canada and that the details of the humour can change from nation to nation, let alone reserve to reserve.

First, Native humour can be extremely self-deprecatory. We love to make fun of ourselves as individuals or as a group. Second, teasing is universal in rez country. Oftentimes you don't know you've been accepted into a community until you've been teased. It's even got an anthropological name: permitted disrespect.

Perhaps nobody is better at self-deprecatory humour than Cree funnyman Don Burnstick. Coming out of the windswept prairie of Alberta, Don became famous (as famous as a Canadian Cree comedian can get) by culturally appropriating a routine made famous by American comedian Jeff Foxworthy. Foxworthy made a name for himself as a "redneck" comedian—often a derogatory term for American southerners. It should be noted that he is a southern man making fun of other southern people. One of his most well-known and funny jokes:

> "If you go to family reunions to meet women, you just might be a redneck."

Now, if somebody outside his sphere of knowledge were to make that joke, it would undoubtedly be deemed politically incorrect. But because Foxworthy is from the South himself, it is legitimate. Burnstick takes that line of humorous thought and indigenizes it. Except this time, it's the pejorative "redskin" instead of "redneck." A subtle but distinctive difference. And again, it's well within Burnstick's particular sphere of knowledge.

> "If you know how to fillet baloney, you just might be a redskin."

> "If you list your probation officer as a reference, you just might be a redskin."

If a non-Native person were to make either of these jokes, there's a good chance a complaint would be made to the Human Rights

Commission, even for simply using the term "redskin." On a similar note, African-Americans retain the right to use the term "nigger," and very few outside that specific sphere of knowledge could get away with using it. It's highly unlikely that even somebody on the same level of the Ladder of Status, like a Native person, could legitimately use that term.

Occasionally, the concept of political incorrectness does rear its head within the confines of the Aboriginal sphere of knowledge. Several years back, in that politically incorrect town known as Winnipeg, a Native community theatre company called Red Roots produced a play entitled *Those Damn Squaws,* which dealt with the issue of being a Native woman in Canada. Evidently the play was quite successful; both Native and non-Native audiences thought it was funny and insightful. All except for one Native man: he filed a complaint with the Manitoba Human Rights Commission. He objected to the word "squaws" in the play's title. He found it derogatory to Native women, and he couldn't understand why a collective of Native women would use it.

How can Natives make fun of white people, though, if their spheres of knowledge are different? Again, keep in mind that humour moves up the ladder, and it's often based on invisible observation (the ability to look without being seen, to observe without being acknowledged). Since there are so many more non-Natives floating around in the world, and non-Native society surrounds us, it's not difficult to come away with at least a superficial knowledge of the dominant culture. By contrast, unless specifically inclined, white people have a limited concept of Native or Chinese or Hindu life, outside the occasional restaurant meal or movie.

A similar model might be Canadians in Hollywood. It's often been asked why there are so many successful Canadians in the American comedy business—witness the careers of former cast

members of *Saturday Night Live* or SCTV and individual comedians like Jim Carrey, Mike Myers and Leslie Nielsen. One
theory has it that by coming from Canada, these comics have
the opportunity to observe American culture from the outside. Because of American cultural dominance, their sphere of
knowledge grows to include the United States. By contrast, the
American knowledge of Canada remains constant at the level of
Mounties, hockey players and polar bears.

In the past fifteen or so years I have written more than two
hundred articles on various aspects of being Native in Canada.
I've written about a dozen plays that comment on Native/non-
Native interaction. White people, the dominant culture, the
colonizers—however you want to put it—often come under my
magnifying glass. (Being half white gives me a certain advantage, though ironically I know practically nothing about that
side of my heritage. My sphere of knowledge has a wedge missing.) In the four published volumes of my articles can be found
some of my most satiric and critical comments—the kind, no
doubt, that the young man in Ottawa found offensive.

Paraphrasing F. Scott Fitzgerald's famous quote about the
rich being different from you and me: "It's been my Ojibway-
tainted observation over the years that middle-class white
people are different from you and me. Yeah, they're insane."

"And on the white hand, there's the concept of breast implants.
Darn clever, them white people. That's something Indians
would never have invented, seriously. We're not ambitious
enough. We just take what the Creator decides to give us, but
not the white man. And let's face it, we know it was a white
*man* who invented them, don't we?"

On why I've been known to date white women: "Let's face it.
White women are easier to find in the dark. And white goes

with any outfit. But I never, ever date a white woman after Labour Day. It's simply not done." (Substitute "white men" in this joke if desired.)

Are these jokes politically incorrect? That's a good question. I wrote them based on observation and participation. My sphere of knowledge enveloped them. The first comment grew out of an article I wrote about white-water canoeing and sea kayaking. It dealt with how so many white people like to taunt death using traditional Native equipment like canoes and kayaks. Most Native people don't do quasi-suicidal things like that. I spent a weekend engaging in these sports as research, so I knew whereof I was writing. The second joke also comes from years and years of observation. In all my travels, I've only met one Native woman who had breast implants. She also had platinum blonde hair, so I think it might have been an overall look she was going for, one that's too high-tech for most Native women. And as most Native women know, having oversized boobs can make you tip the canoe.

Several years ago I wrote a play called *The Bootlegger Blues.* It's about a fifty-eight-year-old good Christian woman who, through a series of circumstances, finds herself in possession of 148 cases of beer that she has to bootleg to buy an organ for the church. The premise itself might be considered politically incorrect—a comedy about Native people bootlegging beer? In fact, one of the jokes dealt with a young man named Andrew, who everybody called Blue because of an embarrassing childhood accident. Another character, a burnt-out partier named Noble, comments when he hears Andrew's nickname: "Hey, cool, you named him after a beer!" Native people roared with laughter at that joke, but white audiences were reluctant. Given the well-publicized alcoholism problems many whites believe exist in every Native community, it was unfathomable that somebody would write something funny about such an issue. And then expect them to laugh at it. During intermission I heard one woman say, "I guess it's funny. But if a white person had written that, he'd be in deep trouble." Again, that sphere of knowledge. That time around, the sphere of knowledge was even bigger than you'd normally expect, because the story was based on an incident that actually happened (or for legal reasons, may not have happened) on my reserve.

Despite all the thinking I've done about graphs and pyramids and spheres of knowledge, there are still times I have to grapple with an ambiguous "politically incorrect" moral dilemma. One occurred recently in my own house. I caught an intriguing episode of *The Simpsons,* a show no stranger itself to skateboarding the line of political correctness. In the episode, for some reason I forget, local children had been polarized into two competing groups. For some reason that escapes my memory, one group, headed by Homer Simpson, were little Indians, dressed appropriately. The other group, headed I believe by Ned Flanders, were little cavalry scouts, also dressed appropriately.

It was a cute episode, especially to a Native person. During one of the challenges, Ned's group wins and one of the kids yells victoriously, "Yeah, the cavalry wins one for once!" The irony was not lost on me. But it was another joke that gave me pause. Homer, dressed as an Indian chief, is sitting on the couch in the living room, watching television, with a beer in his hand. The kids are getting restless. They want to do something and they are trying to convince Homer to lead them. He relents. As he does, the ever-observant Marge says something to the effect of, "Good, I didn't think Indians just sat around watching television and drinking beer."

I was amazed. One thing *The Simpsons* is famous for is comically inverting a statement, saying one thing but meaning another. And that's the impression I got from that line. I didn't know if I should be outraged and insulted. Then I realized I was sitting there on the couch, watching television, with a glass of wine in my hand. I later contacted my friend Don Kelly, a Native comedian and rabid *Simpsons* fan, to see if he had seen the episode.

Don told me he had indeed seen the episode. He remembered the line I was referring to. He too had had a moment of indignation at the implication—until he realized he was sitting on the couch drinking a beer. He had to decide whether to be outraged or amused, and since it's always more fun to be amused, he enjoyed a good belly laugh.

You can always be politically correct tomorrow.

— **NOTES** —

1  Quotes by Paula Gunn Allen and Ward Churchill are taken from *Indi'n Humor: Bicultural Play in Native America* by Kenneth Lincoln (New York: Oxford University Press, 1993).

*Astutely* selected ETHNO-BASED
examples of CULTURAL *jocularity* and
*racial* COMICALNESS

. . . . . . . .

{ EXAMPLE 4 }

A WHITE MAN *hunting geese manages to bag a big one, but it lands behind a barbed-wire fence. When the man gets to the fence he sees a sign that says "Territory of the Jackrabbit Cree Nations." He also sees this old Cree man picking up the goose he shot.*

*"Hey, that's mine," yells the hunter.*

*"I got it first," says the old man.*

*"But I shot it!" exclaims the hunter.*

*"It landed on my territory," says the old man. "Didn't you see the sign?"*

*The hunter is stumped. He offers money. The old man declines. He pleads, but the old man is unmoved.*

*"There's gotta be some way to settle this," says the hunter.*

*"Well, now that you mention it, there is a traditional Cree way of sorting this out," says the old man. "But you've got to promise to follow the rules."*

*The hunter agrees. The old man then says that the way to settle the dispute is by posing a test of strength, stamina and guts. Basically, one person gets three free strikes against the other, and this continues until someone gives up.*

*"Sound okay to you?" asks the old man.*

*"Sure," says the hunter.*

"Since this is my territory, I get to go first."

"Okay," says the hunter, thinking he could handle any strike from the old man. That is, until the first strike, which is a kick to the nuts. The hunter drops like a sack of mud. As he's catching his breath, the old man fires a kick into the hunter's solar plexus. The hunter is gasping for air, the pain intense, until the old man's final kick knocks out half his teeth.

It takes a while, but the hunter finally manages to stand, relishing the chance to get some payback. "Are you ready?" he asks the old man.

"That's okay," says the old man. "You win. I give up. You can have the goose." With a pleased smile, he saunters off into reserve territory.

{ EXAMPLE 5 }

AN INDIAN MAN *found himself in a brothel in Toronto and decided to approach a prostitute. He asked her, "How much do you charge for the hour?"*

*"A hundred dollars," she replied.*

*"Do you do Indian-style?"*

*Not knowing exactly what that was, the woman refused.*

*The man tried to sweeten the deal. "I'll pay you three hundred to do it Indian-style," he said.*

*Again the woman declined.*

*Being the persistent type, the man laid down his final offer. "I'll give you five hundred dollars to go Indian-style with me. What do you say?"*

*The woman thought, "Well, I've been in the game for over ten years now. I've been there and done that, and had every kind of request from weirdos from all over the world. How bad could Indian-style be?" So she finally agreed.*

*After an intense hour of every possible way and position, the woman turned to the man and said, "Well, your time is up, but I was expecting something perverted and disgusting. Where does the 'Indian-style' come in?"*

*The man opened a can of beer and replied, "I'll pay you next Wednesday when I get my welfare cheque."*

{ EXAMPLE 6 }

THREE GUYS WERE *drinking in a bar: a white guy, a black guy and a Native guy. They got drunk and then decided to drive home. They got into a car accident, and all three of them died and went to Hell. The Devil was waiting for them. He told them that he would let them take the stairway to Heaven, but only if they each offered him something of value. So the white guy told the Devil that he could offer the hundred thousand dollars he had in the bank. The Devil was like, "Okay, you can take the stairway."*

*Next, the black guy went up to the Devil and said, "I'm not a rich man, but I do have five thousand dollars in the bank." The Devil thought about it, but then he said, "Okay," and let the black guy go.*

*The black guy caught up to the white guy on the stairway to Heaven, and the white guy said, "Where's the Native guy?" The black guy said, "Oh, he's still back there, trying to convince the Devil that Indian Affairs will cover it."*

# CREE-ATIVELY SPEAKING

..............................

{ JANICE ACOOSE & NATASHA BEEDS }

*For Blair, Blue, Nicole, Alijah, Angelina, Dakota and Rose:*
*So they'll always remember the power of storied humour*
*And for the jazz-man Lee Kozak and the*
*word-mistress Susan Dawson: For their special gifts!*

— IN THE BEGINNING —

TWO FINE *specimens of mixed-Cree womanhood are jog-*
*ging on the treadmills at Mecca Fitness Centre. Janice*
*is training for her 5K race; she is, after all, the grand-*
*daughter of the famous runner Paul Acoose: Man Standing*
*Above Ground. Right next to her, Tasha, her training partner, is*
*just trying to keep up. Tasha is, on the other hand, the grand-*
*daughter of Man Who Smokes Too Much: John Beeds.*

JANICE: Hey, Tasha, wanna write something funny with me
about the Crees?

TASHA: Ho-leeee! Little mixed-blood me? Ahhh goooo onnnn,
you. You really want me to write something with you?

JANICE: Well, our "Blue-Eyed Ojibway" buddy Drew asked me to
write something funny about them Crees, so I thought I better bring along a Cree. You're mixed-blood Cree, aren't you?

TASHA: Yup, my mother is a mixed-blood *Nehiyaw* who fell in love with a woman-lovin' Caribbean man my Granny called "Blue Beard." When he broke my mother's heart, she fled the ocean and mountains and came back to the bush toting me, her Cree-ibbean daughter. But I guess, like a whole buncha other indigenous folks, we're a soup pot of status Cree, non-status Cree, Métis-Cree and just plain Indians. Are *you* Cree, Janice?

JANICE: W-e-l-l, hmm. I don't really tell too many people, but I guess I'll have to fess up sooner or later. You see, I think there was a Cree or two sneakin' around w-a-y back when my down-*Koochum*'s family lived in St. Eustache, Red River.

TASHA: Chaaaa! Why is your *Koochum* down?

JANICE: No, no—she's not down! We called her down-*Koochum* 'cause she lived down the hill from my Grandma's house at the halfbreed colony in Marival.

TASHA: Ooooh! Hey, did your mom's family *really* come from the Red River?

JANICE: Yeah.

TASHA: Ho-leee! You're a *real* Métis then, eh?

JANICE: Well, that's a bit confusing.

TASHA: Why?

JANICE: See, *Ni'mosom*—that's my dad's dad—told us stories about our Anishinabe side of the family for as long as I can remember. So I'm pretty certain about that part of me, but my so-called Métisness, well, that's kinda a contentious issue right now, what with all the bullshit Métis politics goin' on. And gee, if Grandma—that's my mom's mom—ever heard that I was spilling the beans about our Cree connection… well, ho-leeee, she'd be rolling over in her grave. Though, come to think of it, I always wondered why her and my mom's French was peppered with Cree-sounding words, eh? Oh well, guess she didn't nickname me *La'Bishon* for nothing!

TASHA: Chaaaa... *La Ba* what?

JANICE: *La'Bishon*—I think it's some kind of Mitchef-French for "The Big Mouth."

## — CREE-ATIVE CONNECTIONS —

TASHA *(in between puffs)*: Cree humour, eh? *(Puff, puff.)* So, where are we *(puff, puff, puff)* gonna start?

JANICE *(not one single puff)*: Well, the Cree-ator of the world is Wesakaychuk.

TASHA: Eeeee... Don't you know, you can't say His name. It's past springtime!

JANICE: Whaddya mean, you can't say His name?

TASHA: You can only say His name in the winter. If you say it any other time...

JANICE: Ah, go on, don't be silly. Nothin' will happen.

TASHA: Yes, those old people say snakes will come. Don't you remember last year when we were walking and talking about Him and right there, in the middle of that westside road, I saw a snake?

JANICE *(chuckling)*: Yeah, Tasha, I remember. It was a stick, not a snake, but you sure did scream. I bet those hoity-toity folks probably heard you all the way over on the eastside.

TASHA: Okay, okay, maybe it was just a stick, but don't say His name now.

JANICE: Pa-leez. I don't believe in all that old Cree superstitiousness. *Wesakaychuk, Wesakaychuk, Wesakaychuk, Wesakaychuk, Wesakaychuk, Wesakaychuk, Wesakaychuk.* See, nothing happened to me.

*Aghast at Janice's courage, Tasha covers her ears. In seconds, her body is somersaulting through the air. Sounds of terrifying screams are cut short by a* t-h-u-m-p! *As she lands ass over treadmill, Tasha's mixed-blood Cree derrière dangles over the treadmill's rubber. Janice peers mischievously at her with a Trickster-like ear-to-ear smile.*

TASHA *(groaning and moaning over the treadmill's lightning-fast humming)*: Owwwwww! Owwwww! Owww! See, I tolddd you.

JANICE *(laughing uncontrollably)*: Oh god, I'm gonna pee myself.

TASHA: Help me up, you spoon! See, you gotta call Him *Kistasinow* or *Chakapas* or *Ti Jean*…just not the W-word.

JANICE *(still laughing)*: I think maybe you saw stars, not snakes. Anyway, I think you'll be okay if we just write about Him.

TASHA: Yeah, okay, but there's no way I'm gonna read his name out loud!

Along with the stories told around kitchen tables and evening fires, the Trickster was brought onto the cultureless white pages of books in the early 1900s. He is just as powerful on the written page as she is in the oral stories. (Remember, the Trickster is a shape-shifter and has no fixed gender.) Makes sense that she would follow us onto the written page, since wherever we *Nehiyaw* go, the Trickster follows. Yup, her powerful energy illuminates the Cree-ative tales that live between the pages of contemporary written stories. Kicking ass, the Trickster's spirit empowers today's *Nehiyaw* writers to Cree-atively transform the old stories into lily-white words with picket-fence sentences and manicured paragraphs that back-talk the Great White Way of writing, as writer Marilyn Dumont says. With the spirit of the Trickster guiding them, Cree-ative writers bring the humour of the people back from the bush and into the cities. Just wait until those hoity-toity eastsiders see who their next-door neighbour is.

JANICE: Oh! I'm so excited by all this Cree-ativity!

TASHA: Me too, Janice. Cree-ative humour is spilling off the pages of written stories so fast it's drenching "Indian" myths and making mud puddles out of the mastery of English.

Don't ya just love playin' in the mud? The Trickster does.

Just as he reconstructed the world after the great flood, the Trickster reconstructs the world of written English with Cree-ative humour that calls up ancestral spirits and powerful mythological beings. The Trickster uses Cree-ative humour to mirror collective memory, dissolve into digestible laughter centuries-old constipated pain, anoint salve over unhealed wounds and turn the stresses of contemporary living and fast-moving city life into: NEHIYAW TIME!

Hey, Janice, do you *Nehiyaw*-Métis know what time and space that is?

JANICE: Hey, are you trying to Cree-centricize me?

TASHA: Who, little Cree-ibbean me? Never.

I got an idea. Let me show you what I mean by telling you about this short piece I just finished reading. Paul Seesequasis, the guy who wrote it, definitely moves through *Nehiyaw* time. In "The Republic of Tricksterism" (nope, not Plato's *Republic*), Seesequasis Cree-ates a contemporary Trickster story that resurrects our *Nehiyaw* humour, taunts the Cree-centric voice of storytelling, collapses myths into each other and tickles the funny out of seemingly unfunny situations.*

JANICE: Hey, I read it too, Tash. What struck me about that powerful piece is the way that it lies so quiet and unassuming in Daniel David Moses and Terry Goldie's *Anthology of Canadian Native Literature in English*. It stimulated and frustrated me so much that I phoned up Seesequasis and told him so. I told him that I like the way he teases the funny

---

\* Paul Seesequasis, "The Republic of Tricksterism." In *An Anthology of Canadian Native Literature in English*, 2nd ed., eds. Daniel David Moses and Terry Goldie. Toronto: Oxford University Press, 1998. Quotations from the story appear throughout this conversational essay.

right out of the cultural dis-ease so many of us find ourselves drowning in. And the way he un-dams Cree-ative Trickster humour and uses it to wash over the pages.

But mostly I like the way his humour tickles all those ridiculous ideas of Cree cultural purity and pokes fun at our fancy academic writing. Look what happens when he calls up Wesakaychuk, Pakakos, Hairy Hearts, Wetigoes and the Little People. Those figures of Cree oral mythology nonchalantly saunter onto the book's pages and create pandemonium by destabilizing the tightly structured written English. Really, he's very much like the Trickster because he ruptures any potentially fixed interpretations of culture and story. Seesequasis even Tricksterizes our expectations of the Trickster. Remember how he invites the mixed-blood Uncle Morris onto the pages? Morris shape-shifts into the mythical *rigoureau* of Métis oral stories in places where we expect Wesakaychuk to appear. And look at the way Seesequasis uses Cree-ative humour to rip open the seams of the written story. With Trickster energy, the oral storytelling voices break free.

TASHA: Oo! Oo! I just love being teased and tickled. And hey, Janice, did you notice that when Seesequasis assembles his motley crew of characters he whirls his Trickster voice, blowing wind and creating havoc in both the English written form and Cree storytelling? Take the Cree urban mixed-blood orphans, for example. When they make their appearance in his story, they've been de-Cree-d and banished from the so-called Reserve-d Place of Indian culture and storytelling. Fallen between the cracks of mainstream and Cree culture, the urban mixed-bloods become prisoners tangled in the red tape of bureaucracy.

Seesequasis reminds us that both the Reserve-d Place and the Indian have been colonially manufactured by that same government bureaucracy. And his Republic of Trick-sterism alludes to the massive government marketing of both these ideas, constructs that have been bought into by many Cree people ourselves. 'Course I'm talking about the ones Seesequasis says get paid the big bucks, who become Indian clones ready to defend their tribalism and prevent *Nehiyaw* who are not willing to turn Tricks to set foot on the sacredly served lands.

Getting back to the Republic's mixed-bloods, as orphans of the Cree oral storytelling traditions and de-Cree-d out-casts without status in the English written stories, they exist in a storytelling limbo, where both written and oral forms become Tricksterized.

JANICE: What are you talking about, *Tricksterized?* Do you mean like when you tripped over your mouth and ended up with your mixed-blood Cree derrière up in the air?

TASHA: Yeah, yeah, yeah, *La'Bishon.* Just never mind about that. You should see my cheeks. I got big blue bruises from that one.

Anyway—hey! Are you listenin'? As a contemporary writer, Seesequasis uses the English written form, but he re-Cree-ates oral storytelling techniques within his text. Let me show you what I mean. You know that when us *Nehi-yaw* tell *tahp-acimowina* (a true/family story), we introduce ourselves, tell where we come from and who we come from. But when Seesequasis re-Cree-ates this storytelling tech-nique, he uses the Master's tools to dismantle the Master's rules. Appearing to adhere to biographical form, he places the life story of his mother onto the page. According to those written conventions, he writes that she was born on Beardy's Reserve on January 20, 1934, and that her parents are Sam Seesequasis of Beardy's and Mary Rose Nahtowenhow of the Sturgeon Lake band.

Then he Tricksterizes our expectations of form. Using Cree-ative humour he jump-starts these silent written facts into storytelling images: Sam becomes *Nimosom* and starts dancing through the pages with gentleness and humour, and Mary Rose becomes *Nohkom* who shifts into a bear, hunts rabbits, cuts the heads off chickens and farts in the direction of bureaucrats and posers. As literal relatives of the Cree-ative storyteller, *Nohkom* and *Nimosom* disrupt the neatly organized structure of the written word and awaken the senses to the possibilities of cultural differences.

When Tobe, the "grand-chief-to-be," appears on the page alongside figurative beings such as the Trickster and Pakakos, his presence signals the shift from storytelling to the written narrative. Usually, the Trickster and Pakakos signal an oral form, but again we have been Tricksterized. In Seesequasis's text, Tobe's life sits silently factual. He is a mixed-blood, spawned by a Cree father and a white mother, but he grows up as if he is a mixed-race *pure* blood. Exaggerating his half a cup of tribal blood, he thinks himself purer Cree than Mary Seesequasis. Unlike Mary, Tobe has no relations on the written page. His identity flows from the Indian Act. Yup. He is a puffed-up Indian-Act(ing) Indian. On the other hand, the Trickster, Pakakos, Wetigoes and Hairy Hearts are spirited beings relative to Cree *acimowina*. Although they lie quietly on the page as names of remembered stories, they tantalize us with the prospect of things to come.

Teasing and tickling our expectations, the voice of Cree *acimowina* seems tamed by the inherent patriarchal conventions of written English. But when Seesequasis's mother Mary becomes Dennis Ogresko's *hisqueau*, Cree-ative humour puns the English word "his" with the Cree-sounding word "queau" for woman. Think you been Tricksterized again?

JANICE: Maybe a little confused.

TASHA: And when the mixed-blood Uncle Morris shows up as a *rigoureau*, both the forms of oral storytelling and the written tradition evaporate faster than a tin of canned milk. Out of nowhere, spirit rodents and scavengers scamper across the page, escaping the oral realm of Wesakaychuk, Hairy Hearts, the Little People and Wetigoes. In between time, in the meantime, as the storytelling and written narrative voices shape-shift, the story's seams bust ass-wide open. Truth turns into fiction, biblical myths spill into Cree oral telling and Trickster humour rules!

Yeah! I hope that phrase catches on. Oh, baby, *Trickster-ize* me. You've been *Tricksterized*. Let's *Tricksterize*. Kinda has an aerobic sound to it, or maybe it's anaerobic. Knowing the Trickster, it's probably both. But Tricksterizing sure makes us work out hard, eh?

JANICE: Hey, you know it, Tasha. At first I was confused, trying to make sense of Seesequasis's Trickster trickle. It's a good thing I have a bit of Cree-text. Cree-text allows us to appreciate how his mom, Mary, comes to stand in for the oral tradition while the chief functions as a symbol of the written tradition. When Seesequasis plays the two forms of storytelling off against each other, the results are hilarious. How many Cree chiefs do you think would like to be placed in stories between references to *Nohkom*'s smelly farts? Or to materialize in the text smelly with the noxious gas emanating from *Nohkom*'s bowels? But then Tobe is merely a symbolic figure of the de-Cree-ing authority of written narrative. He becomes a colonial clone, selling himself for paper money and papering himself in white, worded definitions and power.

TASHA: Talk about turning Tricks.

JANICE: Yeah, eventually he becomes Grand Chief Tobe in the Fermentation of the Saskatchewan Indian Nations. A rotten chief in a fermenting organization amidst the cultural confusion and ever-increasing number of mixed-bloods moving to the city. Then he becomes the disfigured part-legend part-lie, Honourable Heap Big Chief, after the pronouncement of Bill c-31, the government de-Cree that restored "Indian" status. Like a lot of contemporary skins, the chief imagines himself into being and covers himself with "status." He forgets the oral stories that can speak to him of culture and identity. From the boy who played with the storyteller's mother, Mary, he morphs into the main cannibal spirit who feeds off the flesh of mixed-bloods and urban orphans.

TASHA: Wow, this stuff is really deep. To Cree-textualize his work, Seesequasis embeds it with *wahkotowin*—the strength of relations. Like you said, he places his mother, Mary, in his text as the symbolic figure of Cree cultural traditions of storytelling. Her presence resists the de-Cree-ing authority of the written narrative's masterful conventions. A full-blood *Nehiyaw* woman, Mary is the daughter of *Nimosom* and *Nohkom*. As such, she presides over the story as a familial Cree presence that threatens to rupture the textual surface of written English. And when Mary becomes a *hisqueau* by marrying a white man, she refuses the de-Cree-ing authoritative papers that tell her she is a person without status. Instead of hanging her head in shame when she is exiled from the rez, she re-Cree-ates her own status by becoming a "registered" healer who nurses the ever-increasing community of mixed-bloods and urban orphans. As she shifts her home from Prince Albert to Saskatoon, she shapes the traditional role of healer into an urban "medicine woman" who nurses the whores, dykes, queers and street people at the 20th Street Community Clinic.

JANICE: Tasha, don't you just love Seesequasis's irreverence? He debunks mythic ideas of the sacred. He pokes fun at notions of cultural purity by characterizing the mixed-bloods as urban orphans who have been exiled from the sacred-mythical place of culture: the reserve.

TASHA: And I like the representation of mixed-bloods as resourceful and resilient—like us.

JANICE: Hmm, I wonder if we can call them postmodern non-status urban mixed-bloods? They do, after all, shift the Reserve-d Place of culture by transplanting it into an un-Edenic plot. Shopping malls and beer parlours become their sacred grounds, and Clash-ing–Sex Pistols their tribal drums. Then again, they are outcasts of the constructed written world and orphans of the oral tribal culture, too. Hey, I got it: they're like another shape-shifter between worlds: Wesakay-chuk. They show their irreverence by pissing on city streets to mark shifting traditional territory. As the Trickster's children, they transform ideas of tradition, culture and identity, and they poke fun at clonish Indians. While Indian-Act(ing) Indians roar with anger and smash their fists against their palms, these Trickster upstarts gnaw away at layers of the de-Cree-ing authority.

TASHA: But it's Uncle Morris, the mixed-blood *rigoureau,* who really turns everything upside down. He doesn't pull any punches as he disrespects, even disregards, the boundaries of the de-Cree-d authority. He rambles across the white pages, shape-shifting into the Métis *rigoureau* who then shifts shape into a fictional character named Uncle Morris and then into the legendary Métis activist Malcolm Norris! Blending Métis and Cree *acimowina,* the *rigoureau* Uncle Morris wants to unite all "urban skins" and envisions urban reserves liberated from the Wetigoes and Hairy Hearts. "Free All Urban Skins!" Can't you just hear the rallying cries?

As he shifts the shape of the story form, Uncle Morris parodies the sacred texts of Western civilization. I love how he parodies the Christ stories when he shape-shifts from a squirrel into a Christ-like figure. Of course, he is persecuted and condemned to death for blasphemous challenges to the so-called noble and sacred institutions.

Poor ol' Uncle Morris is nailed to a cross, though in the Cree-text his cross is a metal medicine wheel and his arms and legs are spread in the four directions. Stories are literally turned upside down and around again. In Seesequasis's re-Cree-ated text, Uncle Morris appears as a martyr and saviour dragged before a "regional" council, not the mythic Big Cree Grand Council. Unlike the suffering Christ-martyr, the mixed-blood *rigoureau* doesn't carry his own wooden cross up a rural mountain. No way. This Cree-textualized Christ rolls his cedar-wood wheelchair up the Prince Albert hill.

JANICE: Some of those die-hard Christians are going to take offence at this!

TASHA: Cree-ative humour encourages us to laugh at everything. Nothing is exempt; the more sacred the idea, the better it is to poke fun at. Look at the way Seesequasis pokes fun at both ceremony and ritual. When he writes about Uncle Morris's death, he calls on an urban scavenger crow rather than a majestic eagle to caw his name to the clouds, while memory fires burn in street-corner garbage cans. Uncle Morris rises resurrected, with his Cree-Trickster energy pulsing, not as a holy spirit but as a pesky termite! As that termite, he chews up the pages of the master narratives, spits them out and re-Cree-ates the stories in true Trickster fashion.

JANICE: Even meaning falls apart as the pesky termite chews away at ideas of importance. Yippee! I can't wait to read more re-Cree-ated stories.

— IN THE END —

*Walking towards the change rooms, the two fine specimens of mixed-blood Cree womanhood are glowing and glistening. Heads are turnin' this-a-way and that-a-way.*

TASHA: Wow! I feel awash in that warm fuzzy feeling that comes after a good...

JANICE: Shit!

TASHA: Actually, I was thinking more along the lines of...

JANICE: No, I mean shit, I forgot... I gotta go.

TASHA: Let me guess: that jazz-man is going to soothe you with his smooth-sweet songs.

JANICE: Ohhhh-Lee! I mean Ho-leeee. Okay, I really gotta go.

TASHA: Okay, buddy, nice chattin' with ya.

JANICE: You, too, my friend. Tomorrow? Same place, same time?

# SUBVERSIVE HUMOUR

·······························

*Canadian* NATIVE *Playwrights'* WINNING
*Weapon of* RESISTANCE

·············

{ MIRJAM HIRCH }

*N*ORTH AMERICA'S indigenous peoples have been using humour for centuries. Native humour has remained unnoticed by most settlers until very recently, however. It escaped most historical and literary accounts because the recorders did not perceive the gesture as humorous or did not appreciate the humour. For much of Canadian history, a stern, unyielding profile of the Indian dominated the popular imagination. Indians, it was believed, never laughed.

Even Stephen Leacock, who succeeded Mark Twain as the foremost literary humorist in North America, missed seeing the particular Native sense of humour. In the introductory paragraph of his book on humour, Leacock wrote about Indians:

> On its first settlement from Europe, the outlook for humour in America, and chiefly in New England, looked rather grim. Here on the spot was the Indian, probably the least humorous

character recorded in history. He took his pleasure seriously with a tomahawk. Scientists tell us that humour and laughter had their beginnings in the dawn of history in the exultation of the savage over his fallen foe. The North American Indian apparently never got beyond the start. To crack his enemies' skull with a hatchet was about the limit of the sense of fun of a Seneca or a Pottawottomie. The dawning humour of such races turned off sideways and developed into the mockery and the malice which are its degenerated forms.[1]

The common public failure to perceive Native humour prevailed despite early testimony to the contrary by Washington Irving. Writing about his 1832 trip to the Prairies, Irving declared Indians to be by no means the stoics of the stereotype:

> When Indians are among themselves... there cannot be greater gossips... They are great mimics and buffoons, also, and entertain themselves excessively at the expense of the whites... reserving all comments until they are alone. Then they give full scope to criticism, satire, mimicry, and mirth.[2]

In 1990, Margaret Atwood wrote the following about white ignorance of Native humour:

> There were a lot of adjectives attributed to Native people. Lacking among them was funny. Savage irony and morbid humour did sometimes enter the picture as a kind of self-flagellation device for whites, but on the whole Natives were treated by almost everyone with the utmost gravity, as if they were either too awe-inspiring as blood-curdling savages or too sacrosanct in their status of holy victim to allow of any comic reactions either to them or by them. Furthermore, nobody ever seems to have asked them what if anything they found funny. The Native as presented in non-Native writing was singularly lacking in a sense of humour; sort of like

the "good" woman of Victorian fiction, who acquired at the hands of male writers the same kind of tragic-eyed, long-suffering solemnity.[3]

It was not until the 1960s, notably with George Ryga's *The Ecstasy of Rita Joe*, that Aboriginals and their problems began to be recognized in theatre. Ryga's play makes significant non-Native observations on the life of poverty-stricken inner-city Native people. The stereotyping in *Rita Joe* is bothersome, though, because to be a Native woman in the city is not synonymous with a fate of rape and death. There is no humour in the play, because even the ridiculous scenes that evoke laughter in the audience produce only terror in Rita Joe, or further accentuate her "differentness." The play, like much of Native literature and drama prior to the late 1960s, was about Natives but not written by a Native; it thus imposed a Western world view on Native peoples and cultures and communicated the perspective of a cultural observer rather than that of a participant. This situation changed radically with the social and political upheavals of the late 1960s and early 1970s. The resulting process of decolonization and renewed drive for self-determination sparked the production of literature, the defining characteristic of which is humour, and stimulated the development of a number of Native theatre groups throughout North America.[4] In 1989, author Tomson Highway explained the importance of this development:

> Until we have a generation of Indian people out there who have been inundated with Nanabush stories and incredible literature written by our own people, we won't really have our words as a people, as a distinct culture. Because until that day arrives we are going to continue to be colonised. There are artists who are beginning to speak up now and this colonisation is precisely what the artists growing up today are beginning to change.[5]

The new work being produced by Native writers caused consternation, disbelief and even outrage among non-Natives. As Margaret Atwood notes:

> The comfortable thing about people who do not have a literary voice, or at least not one you can hear or understand, is that you never have to listen to what they are saying about *you*. Men found it very disconcerting when women started writing the truth about the kinds of things women say about them behind their backs. In particular they did not appreciate having the more trivial of their human foibles revealed, nor did they appreciate being laughed at. Nobody does really.[6]

In contemporary Native Canadian literature, theatre is of particular importance. For writers like Tomson Highway, Margo Kane, Marie Clements, Daniel David Moses, Darrell Dennis and Drew Hayden Taylor, drama has become the predominant expressive vehicle and major site of resistance. Theatre provides the possibility of direct confrontation, brings people together, introduces thought-provoking ideas and fosters an openness to dialogue and change. In a 2001 interview, Margo Kane also explained that Native writers prefer drama "because drama is most akin to storytelling."[7]

Contemporary Native theatre stands on a unique historical foundation: a strong tradition of skilled storytelling, the preservation of ritual practices and a new-found literate form of expression.[8] By the time Europeans arrived in North America, every Aboriginal group on the continent had created rituals as part of cultural life. The origins of many contemporary oral comic narratives may be found in religious ceremonies involving sacred clowns and shamans. Ritual clowns, as an integral part of most early Western Native cultures, were privileged to ridicule, burlesque and defile even the most sacred religious festivals. Much of their humour was sexual. In addition, for centuries before European arrival, teasing was used as a method of social control by Native people. Rather than embarrass members of the group publicly, people would tease individuals they considered out of step with the consensus of tribal opinion. Gradually people learned to anticipate teasing and began to tease themselves, as a means both of showing humility and of advocating a course of action they deeply believed in. Like the rituals of the ancient Greeks and Romans, much of what was presented could well be described as theatrical: dance, incantation (plainsong) and the telling and performing of legend and history.[9]

With the arrival of the Europeans, humour became even more important for North America's indigenous peoples. They used it to "make faces" at their colonizers without the latter being able to retaliate. Mohawk actor Gary Farmer explains:

> They needed something that held them together. They had to have the ability to laugh because Native communities have gone through probably the worst of situations in North America that any people have gone through… If they didn't have the ability to laugh they wouldn't be existing today. So humour has been a means of survival, the only means… For the last two hundred years they've had everything taken away from them, their ability to think, practically. Everything: what language they could speak, what religion they could do, and the things they couldn't do. It was all set out for them. All those decisions were taken from them. The only thing they had was their ability to laugh their way through life because if they didn't they would vanish.[10]

Native writer Vine Deloria asserts that humour permeates virtually every area of Indian life—"Nothing in Indian national affairs is possible without it," he says—and that people are frequently educated and "made militant by biting, activist humour."[11]

Contemporary Native authors skilfully employ subversive humour as an artistic strategy both to heal from and to understand historical and personal trauma and to fight the adversity they face. Humour is a means of drawing attention to a range of serious issues, from the perpetuation of stereotypes to land claims, residential schools, forced integration, foster parenthood, benighted government policy, environmental destruction and attempted annihilation. With the help of the strong forces of humour, Native writers challenge given power systems, lay open the relativity of all positions, subvert the processes of domination, inspire social change and promote a new consciousness.

In the foreword to his play *The Baby Blues*, Drew Hayden Taylor explains:

> After many decades of seeing the media highlight the image of the "tragic" or "stoic" Indian, I felt Native people, and consequently non-Native people, were being given a raw deal. I know far more laughing First Nations people than depressed ones. I felt this disproportionate representation had to be addressed. Thus, The Blues Quartet is a series of plays that have their roots in the belly laughs of the communities. And in our history.[12]

Taylor, who has occasionally been referred to as the Neil Simon of Native theatre, says elsewhere that he got "tired of being oppressed and seeing Native women raped on stage."[13] In a newspaper interview, Taylor commented:

> I think the way I write is a result of my upbringing—growing up on the reserve, I was surrounded by this marvellous sense of humour. I have a reputation as a humorist but I am no match to some of my uncles and aunts. Even in the darkest moments there were always sparks of humour. I think

that's how we survived 500 years of oppression. It was our humour that kept us sane. That does not mean that I am using humour to whitewash the problems of Native communities. You can have humour and explore serious issues."[14]

Native plays are often rooted in reality, and many of the stories they tell come from real incidents. Tomson Highway explains:

It's real life. And so when you laugh you know exactly well that you're laughing at death. Real death. So there is this tradition of humour, of an awful lot of funniness, and then there is this history of death. And when the two combine you get a power in the work; that is, it moves into another dimension. It makes it transformational. It creates a metamorphosis in the reader, if the reader can understand what's said and what's not being said.[15]

In Highway's *The Rez Sisters*, a play about the collective quest of seven Native women to attend the "biggest bingo in the world," the character Zhaboonigan describes the incident of an awful rape to the trickster Nanabush, who appears in the form of a seagull:

Are you gentle? I was not little. Maybe. Same size as now. Long ago it must be? You think I am funny? Shhh. I know who you are. There, there. Boys. White boys. Two. Ever nice white wings, you. I was walking down the road to the store. They ask me if I want a ride in car. Oh, I was happy I said, "Yup." Took me far away. Ever nice ride. Dizzy. They took all my clothes off me. Put something up something up inside me here. *Pointing to her crotch, underneath her dress.* Many, many times. Remember. Don't fly away. Don't fly away. Don't go. I saw you before. There, there. It was a. Screwdriver. They put the screwdriver inside me. Here. Remember. Ever

lots of blood. The two white boys. Left me in the bush. Alone.
It was cold. And then. Remember. Zhaboonigan. Everybody
calls me Zhaboonigan. Why? It means needle. Zhaboonigan.
Going-through-thing. Needle Peterson. That's me. It was the
screwdriver.[16]

This episode reflects the gang rape and murder of seventeen-
year-old Helen Betty Osborne in Lac Brochet, Manitoba, by four
young white men. In *The Rez Sisters,* humour is often used in
the women's conversation to deal with the pain that inevitably
accompanies poverty and marginalization:

> PELAJIA: Philomena. Park your tongue. My old man has to
> go the hundred miles to Espanola just to get the job. My
> boys. Gone to Toronto. Only place educated Indian boys
> can find decent jobs these days. And here I sit all broken
> hearted.
>
> PHILOMENA: Paid a dime and only farted.[17]

## — HUMOUR AS A WEAPON —

IT IS NOT EASY to define exactly what characterizes Native
humour. This is not surprising if one takes into account that at
contact fifty-three Native languages were spoken. All nations
have different ways of looking at reality, and these are reflected
in different ways of expressing humour.[18] The Iroquois and the
Haida, for example, are known for aggressive humour, and the
humour of the Cree and the Anishinabe is so sly that "you often
only realize that it was a joke when they start laughing themselves."[19] However, there are two universal factors in Native
humour. One is the strong tradition of teasing. The other is the
self-deprecatory joke told at one's own expense. Drew Hayden
Taylor, for instance, labels himself a NAIFNI ("Native/Aborigi-
nal/Indigenous/First Nations/Indian")[20] and jokes about the
need to found his own nation:

This is a declaration of independence, my declaration of independence. I've spent too many years explaining who and what I am repeatedly, so as of this moment, I officially secede from both races. I plan to start my own separate nation. Because I am half Ojibway, and half Caucasian, we will be called the Occasions. And I, of course, since I'm founding the new nation, will be a Special Occasion.[21]

Some Native writers working with humour incorporate the auditory quality of Native languages and interchange Native languages and English in their texts. In Cree, Tomson Highway explains, humour is embedded in the language itself:

Humour is not understandably present in the words; it can only strongly be sensed in the melody of the Cree language. For a non-Native reader/audience, the hearing of the Cree language is a defamiliarizing experience that causes a heightened awareness of word independent currents, the atmosphere created by sounds and voice... The Cree culture is hilarious. The language that grew out of that mythology is hilarious. When you speak Cree you laugh constantly.[22]

Laughter as a human reflex is unique in that it has no apparent biological purpose. Some scientists have called it a "luxury reflex."[23] On the physiological level, laughter does not require the intervention of the higher mental functions. Emotions and sensations can often generate the bodily movement of laughter before thinking takes place. This separation between thought and emotion creates room for self-reflection and can upset preconceived notions. It is here the "dangerous" power of humour lies.

As Margaret Atwood argues, a person with a sense of humour can never be fully dominated, even when imprisoned, for with the ability to laugh comes a measure of freedom—if not of movement, at least of thought. "Humour is more than a mere tool but becomes an effective subversive weapon, when used by people who find themselves in a tight place without other, more physical weapons."[24]

The subversive humour used by Native playwrights works subtly to communicate an important message and to change beliefs. As Atwood says, plays such as these "ambush the reader. They get the knife in, not by whacking you over the head with their own moral righteousness, but by being funny."[25]

— TRICKSTER HUMOUR —

AT THE CENTRE of much Native mythology stands the Trickster, sometimes described as the "Native version of Jesus,"[26] a being for whom human existence is not a struggle for redemption but a joyous celebration.[27]

Among many First Nations, Trickster stories "were used to teach cultural truths."[28] Depicted as an unrealistic, expressionistic and supernatural figure, half hero, half fool, the Trickster (also called Raven, Bluebird, Nanabush, Napi, Glooscap, Wisakedjak, Hare, Coyote and other names) exhibits a range of contradictory characteristics and qualities: good and evil, male and female, human and animal, creative and destructive, sacred and profane. He/she is the creator and the destroyer, the humorous rogue, the clown, as well as the cynical, malicious swindler and impostor who, with no concept of moral or social values, follows his/her passions and appetites.[29]

In an article by Mac Linscott Ricketts for the journal *History and Religions*, Andrew Wiget summarizes Trickster humour:

> The trickster is the embodiment of humour—all kinds of humour. He plays trickster on others. He ridicules sacred customs, he breaks taboos, he boasts when he should blush, he is the world's greatest clown, and he can laugh at himself. For the religious viewpoint which the trickster represents,

laughter has a religious value and function. In laughing at the incredible antics of the trickster, the people laugh at themselves. The myths of the trickster enabled the Indians to laugh off their failures in hunting, in fighting, in romance, and in combatting the limitations imposed upon them by their environment.[30]

Christian missionaries censored the Trickster as paganistic. Native writers like Tomson Highway, contrary to those who say the Trickster left the continent when the whites came, believe that Canada's Native people have abandoned the Trickster "to drift in the alien, commercialized society around them." Highway considers it the responsibility of the artist to breathe new life into the Trickster, "[who is] passed out under some bar table at Queen and Bathurst, drunk out of his mind, to pitch him off the floor, make him stand up, back on his own two feet—so we can laugh and dance again."[31]

The humour contained within Trickster mythology is complex and culturally distinct. It often evades analysis when removed from its cultural and community context. Although contemporary scholars are aware of this enigma, many early scholars, imposing a Western perspective, contended that the humour in the Trickster myths was "obscene," "crude" or "primitive."[32] The most explicit aspects of Trickster humour can indeed be classified broadly as libidinous and visceral, yet its purpose and function embody a high degree of complexity. Native writer Gerald Vizenor proposes that the Trickster is a semiotic sign and that, as such, Trickster humour represents comic liberation:

> Freedom is a sign and the trickster is chance and freedom in a comic sign; comic freedom is a "doing," not an essence, not a museum being, or an aesthetic presence. The trickster, as a semiotic sign, is imagined in narrative voices, a communal rein to the unconscious, which is comic liberation, however,

the trickster is outside comic structure, "making it" comic rather than "inside comedy, being it." The trickster is agnostic imagination and aggressive liberation, a "doing" in narrative points of view, and outside the imposed structures.[33]

The use of the Trickster by Native writers indicates that Native humour is associated with more than the comic. The audience laughs at the appearance or the funny behaviour of the Trickster, including sight gags or comic fart effects, and at the way the story is told. Yet the story itself is not funny. Only at a second glance does it become clear that the situation is more complex than initially believed, often involving distressing subject matter like rape, suicide or alcoholism.

In Tomson Highway's *Dry Lips Oughta Move to Kapuskasing*, for example, Dickie Bird pulls the trigger of his gun to put an end to his suffering. The gun is not loaded, and Dickie Bird rests immobile facing his father. The trickster Nanabush cuts the complete silence. The production notes direct: "Marilyn Monroe farts, courtesy of Ms. Nanabush: a little flag reading 'poot' pops up out of Ms. Monroe's derriere, as on a play gun. We hear a cute little 'poot' sound."[34]

Highway's play is structured in such a way that the audience laughs at what seem to be the most inappropriate moments. The Nanabush character dances, teases, revels and challenges through exaggerated male and female forms of beauty, grotesqueness and grace, to reorient the audience to a different way of thinking. Other Native playwrights employ similar techniques. Pathetic as some scenes are, the characters and the playwright find a way to live with things by joking. Vine Deloria describes the technique well: "The more desperate the problem, the more humour is directed to describe it."[35] Through burlesque or through wild or obscene humour, the audience can face some of the play's horror with a bravery that otherwise would not be possible. The comic give us the necessary strength to bear the tragedy.

With the help of the Trickster, Canadian Native playwrights have become skilled at representing cultural stereotypes in a humorous, ironic fashion, revealing not only their ideological underpinnings but also how historical misconceptions have hindered cross-cultural understanding and interaction. The Trickster is very important in the genre of resistance literature. With puckish, pointed humour, Native writers explore border zones between Native and European cultures and invite their audiences to see the world in a new way. The Trickster in *Dry Lips* plays hockey. Nanabush in *The Rez Sisters* is both a seagull and a bingo master. The deliberate flouting of decorum and the blending of images from high and low white culture creates a hybrid. In *Dry Lips*, Highway combines mystic jukeboxes, country-and-western songs and an amateur hockey league with evocations of Greek drama and Shakespearean comedy. The strategies and forms of opera are juxtaposed in *The Rez Sisters* with the excitement of a monster bingo. Such conjunctions of the popular and the elite can subtly derail the schooled responses of a mainstream audience, causing them to critically reflect on their own values. This estranging use refuses to accept the cultural products of the dominant society according to that society's estimations.

A corporeal Trickster, however, does not appear in all Native texts. Drew Hayden Taylor states about his plays:

> I cannot tell you how many times I have been asked and answered questions about Trickster influences in my (very little) and other Native writers' (it varies) works. And I can safely say that in these eight stories there was not one single Trickster image, element or appearance made. It seems the future bodes much sadness for non-Native academics.[36]

It is important not to play the game of "Spot the Trickster," which Taylor and fellow playwright Daniel David Moses playfully accuse academics of doing.[37] What *is* important is to recognize the Tricksterish spirit "permeat[ing] almost all work presented as Native theatre."[38] In the foreword to his play *The Baby Blues*, Taylor defines his understanding of the Trickster:

> This wondrous character is a glorious celebration of the mischievous, the joke, the play, and I guess in the end the art of the storyteller. I try to keep true to the Trickster spirit, for I wrote what some have called a Native version of a British sex farce, as a celebration of the aboriginal sense of humour.[39]

The tricksterish spirit in *The Baby Blues* lies in the contradictory take on the relations between white and Native cultures. Taylor's prior concern in the play is to counter the image of the "authentic Indian." *The Baby Blues* makes great fun of whites in search of "authentic Indianness," confronting the white search for the "true" (that is, the vanishing) Indian with thoroughly hybrid real Indians instead. One-sided positive preconceptions, Taylor says, "are as racist as the opposite stereotype of the cruel Indian."[40]

*The Baby Blues* mocks romantic popular-culture notions of the "authentic Indian" in the person of Summer. Summer has lines such as "He's one with Mother Earth and Father Sky."[41] She vehemently denies her whiteness—"Creator forbid, I certainly am not one of them"[42]—instead proudly announcing, "I do consider myself a part of the great aboriginal collective."[43] And she has every reason to do so because she is "part Indian."[44] The exact percentage of her aboriginal heritage is "one sixty-fourth Native."[45] About realizing her dream, she says, "Oh, I hope I have the honesty and spirit to open myself up to these people and show them my purity of heart so they will accept me into their fold...but...but...I must not appear too eager."[46]

White discourse concerning the "authentic Indian" is mimicked by the Native characters themselves. In the first scene of *The Baby Blues*, Summer and the Native Skunk talk together:

SUMMER: Excuse me, but, if you don't mind me asking,
where are you going with the towel. A sweatlodge maybe?
SKUNK: A swim.
SUMMER: Oh. *SUMMER looks disappointed and SKUNK*
*catches this. His attitude changes.*
SKUNK: Ah yes... I'm going for my... morning purification...
cleansing swim, in the lake... Mother Earth's lake... the
tears of Mother Earth.
SUMMER: Really?!
SKUNK: Yes, I do it every morning... to greet our brother
the sun. Right around that bend is a secluded bay where
I... reveal myself to the world, pay homage to the land,
the water and the sun. And wash...[47]

Throughout the play, humour is used to underline deeply serious matters of tradition and cultural assertion. The thoroughly hybrid real Indians are signified by the character Amos's famous "Fortune Scones":

NOBLE: Making some bannock?
AMOS: Kinda. It's a special kind of bannock. I call it Fortune
Scones.
NOBLE: Fortune Scones?
AMOS: Got the idea in a Chinese restaurant. I fry them with
little philosophical Indian sayings in the middle. People
love them.
NOBLE: You're kidding?!
AMOS: No, it sells. White people will buy anything.[48]

Summer's search for authentic Indians is driven by her sense of sharing white guilt for the destruction of the pure

Indian culture of the timeless past, and her desire to do her bit to atone. This combination of white guilt and white ownership of the criteria for authenticity is held up to mockery in the play's opening lines:

> Oh, listen to the children of nature playing, being one with the lake. Oh, it is bliss, sheer bliss. The harmony I feel in this place. Here I am surrounded by trees, flowers, grass, squirrels, and Native people. Tree to tree. First Nations. Aboriginal people in their natural environment.[49]

A few lines later, Summer becomes more explicitly direct:

> No, I admit it, I was raised as a member of the oppressive white majority that is responsible for the unfortunate economic and social conditions your people live in. But really, deep, deep down inside, I'm a good person. Really I am! That's why I took this Native Studies class. Don't blame me for what they have done. I want to atone for their sins.[50]

Summer's behaviour encourages the members of the audience to laugh at themselves in a "comic shock of recognition." Indeed, this is precisely what the Trickster figure does in many Native plays, as Dietmar Kügler asserts: "He holds a mirror up to humanity and has us look at ourselves."[51]

— CONCLUSION —

HUMOUR, always present in Aboriginal oral narratives, has taken on even more important dimensions in the ongoing Native American literary renaissance.[52] Whether confronting annihilation in the physical or in the spiritual sense, the comic tenacity of Native playwrights suggests that the most deeply liberating function of humour is to free others to hope for the impossible. Interviewed at the National Arts Centre in Ottawa, where he was in rehearsal for the role of Zachary Keechigeesik in *Dry Lips*, Gary Farmer expressed:

I love to make people laugh so that I can turn around and make them think. If they laugh, they're going in. They're going deeper. They're falling for the bait. It's like you bait it. It's like bait and you put it out there like a little snare, and they laugh and they laugh, and they're having a good time, and they're really laughing and all of that information is getting in there. You're laying all the groundwork for all that information and then you come across with what you're really [saying]... I mean... the bottom. I mean we're talking about the bottom. It bottoms out and when it bottoms out... it stings there. It burns an image in your brain. It just sits there and it will sit there for a long time. I've seen people come to [this] play and they just can't figure it out. They're moved. Something is different about them from the time they came in [to] when they leave. There's something that burns there, an image that burns there, good or bad, it sits there and it makes them ponder about and think about the condition of these people [on the reserve]... [Still] it's actually, I think, a story of hope... As a human race we've all hit the bottom, and now it's time to move up to where there is hope in the world. We can turn all this around. It doesn't have to be like that.[53]

Canadian Native playwrights are well aware that their audiences will include both Native people and Euro-Canadians. As Tomson Highway explains: "I like to write in such a way that it moves all people, moves rocks. Then I think my job has been done."[54]

How a play is received, however, is subjective, and each audience member's response depends on his or her way of seeing. According to playwright Yvette Nolan, "[The] element of trickster in much Native work... seems to speak to Native audiences in ways that escape or elude white audiences. The knowledge of the trickster and his/her ways creates a common knowledge that is conducive to laughter."[55] Nolan further explains:

What makes it difficult for a non-Native audience to grasp what a Native play really is about is the white gaze. The biggest cultural difference is our history of oppression versus their history as oppressors. And an unwillingness or inability to grasp that concept may make it difficult to truly understand the play. There are other things, of course, cultural differences around humour and structure, but none of these are as insurmountable as a history shared from opposite sides.[56]

Thus the meanings a non-Native audience member derives from Native works may be entirely different from what a Native person finds in them. As one literary critic discovered in analyzing Tomson Highway's work, "non-Natives need to experience these plays in the company of Native audiences to fully appreciate the humour."[57]

Yet as Tomson Highway reminds us, "It is a very basic impulse, the need to communicate, to make people laugh, to make people enjoy and celebrate life."[58] Although everyone might not understand all of the allusions, humorous passages and in jokes in a play, the communal basic idea is still evident. It is a message we should all take to heart, Highway says, because Native writers admonish us: "Please be joyful! Celebrate life, celebrate your families, your friends and your lovers, celebrate the sunlight, the water, the wind, the laughter of strangers, celebrate the very earth you walk on."[59] As Kate Vangen explains: "Making fun— laughing with rather than at—then becomes a way of living with difference."[60]

Subverting the claim to universality made by the dominant cultures, Native playwrights employ this mysteriously powerful weapon, the cross-cultural language of humour. Humour may be nothing new to Native culture. But this use of it surely is. As contemporary Native playwrights demonstrate, humour can bridge two worlds on one stage.

— NOTES —

1. Stephen Leacock, *The Greatest Pages of American Humor*. New York: The Sun Dial Press, 1942, p. 9.
2. John Lowe, "Coyote's Jokebook." In *Dictionary of Native American Literature*, ed. Andrew Wiget. New York: Garland, 1994, p. 193.
3. Margaret Atwood, "A Double-Bladed Knife: Subversive Laughter in Two Stories by Thomas King." *Canadian Literature* 124–125 (March 1990), p. 243.
4. Diane Debenharn, "Native People in Contemporary Native Drama." *Canadian Drama* 14-2 (1988), p. 137.
5. Nancy Wigston, "Nanabush in the City." *Books in Canada* 18-2 (March 1989): p. 8.
6. Margaret Atwood, p. 244.
7. Ginny Ratsoy, "Life and Art in the Creation and Production of Marie Clements' *The Unnatural and Accidental Women.*" In *Playing the Pacific Province: An Anthology of British Columbia Plays, 1967–2000*, eds. Ginny Ratsoy and James Hoffman. Toronto: Playwrights Canada, 2001, p. 413.
8. Beth Brant, *Writing as Witness: Essay and Talk*. Toronto: Women's Press, 1994, p. 39.
9. Hanay L. Geiogamah, "The Native American Theatre." In *Dictionary of Native American Literature*, ed. Andrew Wiget. New York: Garland, 1994, p. 379.
10. Gary Farmer, "The Shame Man: Going Beyond Indian—The Performance Art of James Luna." *Aboriginal Voices* 1-4 (1993), p. 20.
11. Vine Deloria, "Indian Humour." In *Custer Died for Your Sins: An Indian Manifesto*. New York: Macmillan, 1969, p. 147.
12. Drew Hayden Taylor, *The Baby Blues*. Vancouver: Talonbooks, 1999, p. 7.
13. Felicia Hardison Londré and Daniel J. Watermeier, *The History of North American Theater*. New York: Continuum, 1999, p. 78.
14. Jill Lawless, "Humour Is Drew Hayden Taylor's Release." *Now*, April 10, 1996.
15. Gitta Honegger, "Native Playwright: Tomson Highway." *Theater* 23-1 (December 1992), p. 90.
16. Tomson Highway, *The Rez Sisters*. Saskatoon: Fifth House, 1988, pp. 47–48.
17. Tomson Highway, *The Rez Sisters*. Saskatoon: Fifth House, 1988, p. 7.
18. Likewise, the body language of humour and the physical expression of laughter vary from nation to nation. Members of some nations have the ability to laugh with their whole bodies, whereas others express laughter in the chest region or primarily in facial movements.
19. Drew Hayden Taylor, personal interview, May 14, 2002.
20. Drew Hayden Taylor, "The First Annual Aboriginal Trivia Contest," *Further Adventures of a Blue-Eyed Ojibway: Funny, You Don't Look Like One Two*. Penticton: Theytus, 1999, p. 44.
21. Drew Hayden Taylor, "Pretty Like a White Boy: The Adventures of a Blue-Eyed Ojibway." In *An Anthology of Canadian Native Literature in English*, eds. Daniel David Moses and Terry Goldie. Toronto: Oxford University Press, 1998, p. 439.
22. Nancy Wigston, p. 8.

23. Robert McHenry, "Humour and Wit." In *The New Encyclopedia Britannica*, vol. 20, 15th ed. Chicago: Encyclopaedia Britannica, 2002, p. 682.

24. Margaret Atwood, p. 244.

25. Margaret Atwood, p. 244.

26. Robert Enright, "Let Us Now Combine Mythologies: The Theatrical Art of Tomson Highway." *BorderCrossings* 11-4 (December 1992), p. 24.

27. Denis W. Johnston, "Lines and Cyrcles: The 'Rez' Plays of Tomson Highway." *Canadian Literature* 124-125 (March 1990), p. 254.

28. Allan J. Ryan, *The Trickster Shift: Humour and Irony in Contemporary Native Art*. Vancouver: UBC Press, 1999, p. 53.

29. Catherine Mattes, "Trick and Treat." *BorderCrossings* 18-4 (Fall 1999), p. 20.

30. Andrew Wiget quoted in Mac Linscott Ricketts, "The North American Indian Trickster." *History and Religions* 5-2 (1966), p. 347.

31. Tomson Highway quoted in Beth Brant, p. 133.

32. Robert F. Sayre, "Trickster." *North Dakota Quarterly* 53-2 (Spring 1985), p. 73.

33. Gerald Vizenor, "Trickster Discourse." *American Indian Quarterly* 14 (Summer 1990), p. 285.

34. Tomson Highway, *Dry Lips Oughta Move to Kapuskasing*. Saskatoon: Fifth House, 1989, p. 107.

35. Vine Deloria, p. 147.

36. Drew Hayden Taylor, "Native Themes 101." In *Writing Prose: Techniques and Purposes*, 3rd ed., eds. Thomas S. Kane and Leonard J. Peters. New York: Oxford University Press, 1969, p. 7.

37. Drew Hayden Taylor, *Funny, You Don't Look Like One: Observations from a Blue-Eyed Ojibway*, rev. ed. Penticton: Theytus, 1998, p. 88.

38. Drew Hayden Taylor, "The Re-Appearance of the Trickster: Native Theatre in Canada." In *On-Stage and Off-Stage: English Canadian Drama in Discourse*, eds. Albert-Reiner Glaap and Rolf Althof. St. John's: Breakwater, 1996, pp. 51–52.

39. Drew Hayden Taylor, *The Baby Blues*, p. 8.

40. Drew Hayden Taylor, personal interview, January 16, 2002.

41. Drew Hayden Taylor, *The Baby Blues*, p. 53.

42. Ibid., p. 12.

43. Ibid., p. 13.

44. Ibid., p. 14.

45. Ibid., p. 14.

46. Ibid., p. 12.

47. Ibid., pp. 14–15.

48. Ibid., p. 35.

49. Ibid., p. 12.

50. Ibid., p. 13.

51. Dietmar Kügler, "Buchbesprechungen." *Magazin für Amerikanistik* Heft 3 (3. Quartal 1999), p. 43.

52. For a fuller development of what the term means, see Kenneth Lincoln, *Native American Renaissance*. Berkeley: University of California Press, 1983.

53. Gary Farmer, quoted in Allan J. Ryan, p. 169.

54. William Morgan, "The Trickster and Native Theatre: An Interview with Tomson Highway." *Aboriginal Voices: Amerindian, Inuit, and Sami Theater*, eds. Per Brask and William Morgan. Baltimore: Johns Hopkins University Press, 1992, p. 132.

55. Yvette Nolan, quoted in Albert-Reiner Glaap, "Margo Kane, Daniel David Moses, Yvette Nolan, Drew Hayden Taylor: Four Native Playwrights from Canada." *Anglistik Mitteilungen des Verbundes deutscher Anglisten* 7-1 (March 1996), p. 21.

56. Ibid., p. 20.

57. Agnes Grant, "Canadian Native Literature: The Drama of George Ryga and Tomson Highway." *Australian Canadian Studies* 10-2 (1992), p. 50.

58. Tomson Highway, "Dancers for Life: Merely Going Away." *x-TRA* 30 (April 1992).

59. Ibid.

60. Kate Vangen, "Making Faces: Defiance and Humour in Campbell's *Halfbreed* and Welch's *Winter in the Blood*." In *The Native in Literature: Canadian and Contemporary Perspectives*, eds. Thomas King, Cheryl Calver and Helen Hoy. Oakville: ECW Press, 1987, p. 192.

*Astutely* selected ᴇᴛʜɴᴏ-ʙᴀsᴇᴅ

examples of ᴄᴜʟᴛᴜʀᴀʟ *jocularity* and

*racial* ᴄᴏᴍɪᴄᴀʟɴᴇss

. . . . . . . .

{ ᴇxᴀᴍᴘʟᴇ 7 }

ᴡʜᴇɴ ᴛʜᴇ ғɪʀsᴛ *settlers arrived, back several hundred years ago, they made a deal with the local Mi'kmaq. For a set fee, the settlers got a couple miles of land to build their houses on. A small community was built and a trading relationship was set up with the local Native population, who discovered the way things were bought and sold in the Caucasian community. But as is often the way, before you know it these settlers began to breed. More and more of them also showed up on the beaches. It wasn't long before more land was needed. A meeting was quickly established with the local Mi'kmaq. "We need more land," the settlers said.*

*The Mi'kmaq heard the words of their white neighbours and went off to discuss and argue about their request. They came back a few days later. The mighty Mi'kmaq chief approached the leader of the Caucasian community and announced, "We have talked hard and long about this. Some did not want to sell you any more land. Others did. Finally, after much discussion, we came to a consensus. We will sell you more land. But we will sell it to you the same way you sell us things: by the pound."*

## { EXAMPLE 8 }

THREE OJIBWAY MEN *were out hunting one day. As they chased a deer through the bush, they suddenly found themselves surrounded by a dozen Mohawk warriors, their mortal enemies. The Ojibway men were quickly overcome. Tied up, they were carried back to the Mohawk campsite.*

*Once there, the three hunters were bound to posts in the centre of the camp as they awaited their fate. Eventually, close to dawn, the Mohawk chief approached them and spoke of his intentions.*

*"You have been captured. When the dawn comes, you will all be killed, and your skin will be used to make our canoes. But to prove we respect you as fellow warriors and want you to die as men, we will allow you one last request before we kill you."*

*The chief then asked the first Ojibway hunter, "What is your last request?"*

*"I want a woman," the hunter said. "I want to spend my last moments in this life in the arms of a woman." So a woman was brought to him. Soon afterwards, he was killed and his skin was taken to make a canoe.*

*The Mohawk chief went to the second Ojibway and asked, "What is your last request?"*

*"I want to be able to sing my death song," the second man said, "and smudge myself to prepare for my journey into the next world." So the Mohawk chief saw to it that the man was untied and allowed to sing his death song and to smudge. Then he was killed and his skin was taken to make a canoe.*

*The Mohawk chief approached the third and final Ojibway hunter. "What is your last request, Ojibway?"*

*The third Ojibway hunter said, "As my final request, I would like a fork."*

*This time the Mohawk chief was puzzled. "A fork? Why do you want a fork?" he asked of the Ojibway.*

The Ojibway responded, "Will you or will you not grant me my final request?"

Still puzzled, but honouring his promise, the Mohawk chief ordered the Ojibway untied, and the man was brought a fork. The Ojibway took it as the Mohawk chief asked again, "Why did you want a fork?"

The Ojibway hunter quickly started stabbing himself all over his body, puncturing his skin. "No goddamn way you're gonna make a canoe out of me!" he said.

{ EXAMPLE 9 }

A MINISTER IS *walking through the woods with a young Native man. He's attempting to teach the Native how to speak English, so they go from thing to thing as the minister points and speaks the correct name aloud.*

*They approach a large rock. "This is a rock," the minister says. "Rock," says the Native man.*

*They walk on until they come to a tree.*

*"This is a tree," says the minister.*

*"Tree," says the Native man, and they walk on.*

*Eventually they come down to a riverbank. The minister is about to say "river" when they spot a man and a woman having sex on the bank. The minister is surprised and embarrassed. He doesn't know what to say or how to deal with this situation.*

*Finally, recovering, he points to the couple and says, "Man riding a bicycle."*

*Without responding, the young Native man takes out his bow and arrow and puts an arrow in the back of the man lying on top of the woman. The minister is shocked and horrified.*

*"Why... why did you do that?" he asks.*

*"My bicycle," responds the Native man.*

# HOW TO BE AS FUNNY
# AS AN INDIAN

. . . . . . . . . . . . .

{ IAN FERGUSON }

*T*HESE TWO *Indians walk into a bar…*
Well, now, that's not right, is it? First of all, is the word "Indian" even considered correct these days? Let's try that again.

*These two Native North American Aboriginal First Nations Indigenous Peoples walk into a bar…*

Okay, that's a little better. We've used the correct identifying terminology and, uh…umm…damn it. They're going into a bar? That's merely perpetuating a negative stereotype.

*These two Native North American Aboriginal First Nations Indigenous Peoples walk into a sweat lodge…*

Good. Unless…we're not making fun of their religion, are we?

*These two Native North American Aboriginal First Nations Indigenous Peoples walk into a building of some sort or other…*

Hmm…now it doesn't seem all that funny. Still, there's nothing to offend anyone there, and that's the whole point, isn't it?

Actually, no, it's not. Relax. Don't get too worked up. It's just a joke.

That's what this book is about, after all. Humour.

Or, to be specific, Aboriginal humour, a topic that I'm sure has been the subject (or should that be a subject that has been the topic?) of many a doctoral thesis in Cultural Anthropology. Hey: if that isn't funny, I don't know what is.

Aboriginal humour is sometimes described as humour of the oppressed. Certainly it has evolved into a defence mechanism. A lot of First Nations humour is used as a way of dealing with anger and frustration. But humour was a part of Native culture long before first contact. There are traditional ceremonies that incorporate humour, and some of the most vivid creation stories are quite funny. Learning through laughter has been a part of Aboriginal culture since the beginning.

Not that I'm qualified to discuss this. If you're looking for an in-depth analysis of the origins and meanings of First Nations humour, you're going to have to look elsewhere—perhaps in this very book. I'm just guessing—I haven't had the chance to read the book yet, but you have, and that's the most important thing. Me, when I think of Aboriginal humour—and by humour, of course, I mean "jokes"—I think of three categories: Not Jokes, In Jokes and Our Jokes.

— 1. NOT JOKES —

THIS FIRST CATEGORY consists of jokes told about Indians, usually at their expense, by people who are, shall we say, non-Native... or, to be more specific, White People. These are commonly known as "drunken Indian" jokes, and every second one seems to end with the punchline "Oh, no, it's the Breathalyzer again." These kinds of jokes are part of the underground canon known as Bigot Humour, which in itself is an oxymoron, which is kind of funny when you think about it that way. In this day and age almost nobody tells these jokes in public, or even admits to first-hand knowledge of them.

If you've ever told a "drunken Indian" joke, then yes, *sigh*, you probably are a bigot. Except you've already proven that you're not, or, at least, you've made up for it. After all, you bought this book, didn't you? If you are Native, *heavy sigh*, you've already heard all of these jokes. I'm not going to give any examples. They are Not Jokes. It's not just because they are offensive. Much worse: they aren't funny.

— 2. IN JOKES —

THE SECOND CATEGORY of Aboriginal humour consists of jokes told by Indians when non-Natives (and this again refers primarily to White People) are in the room. These jokes tend to be a little self-deprecating, and they often have a political edge to them. Don Kelly, a very funny comedian who just happens to be Aboriginal, does a nice bit in his act about his spirit name being "Dances Without Rhythm." He is, of course, playing with the iconography of the whole *Dances With Wolves* image. Big laugh every time.

These are In Jokes because they allow the listener to feel in on the joke. If you are non-Native, you can pretend to have a deeper understanding of Aboriginal culture than you really do. And you'll appear tolerant. So there is a hip quality to laughing at these jokes; it allows you to indicate that, yes, the First Nations got a really raw deal, but hey, we're all in this together now, and isn't it good that we can all have a bit of a chuckle over what is, really, a serious flaw in Canadian history. Not to mention Canadian culture. Here are some examples of In Jokes:

*Things To Say When Meeting a White Person:*
    "So, just how White are you?"
    "You know, it's funny, but you really don't look all that White."

"I'm partly White myself."

"What do you call that outfit you're wearing? A...sports... jacket? Is that a traditional design?"

"God, I just love your hair, can I touch it?"

"I know all about White culture. When I was in university I took a course in Caucasian Studies."

"Cigarette?"

*or:*

What were Custer's last words? "These Siouxs are killing me."

*or:*

A politician goes to a reserve to give a speech. He tells people that he's from the government and he's there to help them. "Guyoks," his audience murmurs. He says prosperity is just around the corner. Again, the Natives listening to him respond en masse with "Guyoks." With each statement and every promise, the crowd chants "Guyoks," over and over again. The politician has an interpreter with him, and he asks her what the word means. "Don't know," says the interpreter, "must be local vernacular." On the way back to his car, the politician crosses through a cow pasture. "Careful," says the interpreter, "you don't want to step in the guyoks."

*or:*

These two White guys walk into a bar...

The whole point of In Jokes is their accessibility. Everyone is allowed to laugh, and everybody is supposed to get the joke. Despite the social commentary of the subject matter or point of view, no one is meant to feel uncomfortable. If there is a little teasing going on, it's supposed to be gentle, not mean-spirited. Of course, in one of the examples given above, it's helpful if you already know that many First Nations people have difficulty pronouncing the *sh* sound, and would say "shoe" and "Sioux" the same way.

The surprising thing for most non-Natives is that Indians are funny in the first place. In 2001 I was invited to Whitehorse to appear in the Nakai Theatre's Real Millennium Comedy Festival. It was a good time. Brent Butt was the headliner; he's one of Canada's funniest Caucasian comedians. Lorne Elliott, another funny White comic, taped a special edition of his radio show, *Madly Off in All Directions.* I performed as part of the Aboriginal Comedy Night, which was headlined by Sharon Shorty, who is a resident of Whitehorse and one of the funniest women you could ever meet.

Sharon was kind enough to invite a bunch of us over to her house for a big feed of moose-meat stew and a proper visit. She had very few complaints about White People, though she did mention she was tired of being asked to interpret their dreams. The biggest problem she encountered was when she'd tell them what she did for a living. Most of them couldn't get their heads around the idea of a Native comedian. "They think we're serious and spiritual all the time," Sharon said, "which is an improvement over how they used to think about us, but still." I told her that, personally, I felt Kevin Costner had a lot to answer for. Then she and I and Drew Hayden Taylor (the editor of this very book) started riffing.

I should probably mention that Drew was at the festival to present his documentary on Native humour, *Redskins, Tricksters and Puppy Stew.* He was the only one of us getting a per diem, so he really didn't need a free dang meal, but I guess he was there mainly for the conversation. Anyway. The three of us started off trying to make each other laugh, not to mention the other people in the house, and I have to say we came up with some good stuff. It's kind of like when musicians get together: they just can't stop themselves from pulling out their guitars and jamming. It's the same with comedians. Get a group of funny people together and they are just going to start improvising. We can't help it. We were born that way.

The highlight had to be when we started in on the idea of a First Nations Barbie, and how such a doll might be marketed. "New from Mattel, it's First Nations Barbie. Abusive boyfriend Ken and stolen Camaro sold separately." "Coming soon, Second Wife Barbie. Formerly known as Little Sister Stacy." Like that. Poseable and bendable dolls were not a big part of Drew's and my childhood, unless you count "action figures" like G.I. Joe and Johnny West, so it was Sharon who came up with the button. "The problem with a First Nations Barbie would be all those poor factory workers in Taiwan," she said, doing a little mime to make her point. "Can't you see them spending all their time filing down the doll's rear end?" Now maybe you had to be there, but this had everybody in the house in stitches. Well, almost everybody. The one or two people who weren't familiar with the traditional lack of—how to put this delicately—a proper ass in the Indian population looked a little confused. They didn't get the joke.

Which brings us to the third category of Aboriginal humour...

### — 3. OUR JOKES —

DON BURNSTICK, another funny Indian, and a professional comedian to boot, has a good "You might be Aboriginal if... " routine: "You might be Aboriginal if you know thirty-seven ways to prepare Spam," "if you've ever borrowed someone else's false teeth," "if there are three different sizes of tires on your truck and only three legs on your dog." Like that.

The point of Our Jokes is to tell the truth. The humour is less directed outward, towards the dominant culture, than it is focussed on the specificity of the Aboriginal way of life. You know, the day-to-day stuff that really constitutes a culture. It's not that these jokes aren't told in mixed company, though most Indians would hesitate to share them with a completely non-Aboriginal crowd; it's that Our Jokes can be less accessible than

In Jokes, and some sort of translation or explanation is often required. So be prepared. If you wind up in the audience of a comedy show featuring First Nations comedians, you might find yourself missing some of the humour. Unless, again, you are Native, in which case you're going to get the jokes but may have had trouble finding a place to park.

Tomson Highway once opened a speech at Sty-Wet-Tan by remarking that so many people had showed up they should play bingo. Indians are big on bingo. This has everything to do with the Catholic Church, which bears the blame (or the credit) for three or four generations of Aboriginal bingo addicts (not to mention a few other things). The priests were down on traditional Indian games of chance, like pah-kee-shea gambling, not to mention wealth redistribution of any kind, like the potlatch, but they gave an exemption to bingo. You'd need that information to properly appreciate the numerous references to bingo that pop up in First Nations humour. Unless you're Native, in which case you're thinking, "Well, yeah, we like playing bingo, but so what... Everybody knows that already." To which I can only reply, "You're being cheeky, you."

I sign my name "Ian (me)." Not on legal documents or contracts, and not in formal situations, but on letters and cards and e-mails and such. I've done this forever, or at least since I learned to read and write. It comes from growing up in Fort Vermilion, Alberta, where the population was predominantly Bush Cree. That's how everybody talked. "Where you going, you?" "I'm going to the store, me." I never thought anything about it, but it sure leaked into my writing. The oral storytelling tradition that I grew up with—the elliptical narrative, the repetition of words, the self-deprecating humour—has influenced me as a playwright and an author and has become part of how I tell my own stories. If there is anything remotely resembling a style in my work, that's where it comes from.

Here are some examples of Our Jokes:

"What time did you get home last night?"

"I haven't yet."

*or:*

"What's in that paper bag?"

"Bottle of wine for my wife."

"Good trade."

*or:*

"What's the most confusing day on a reserve?"

"Father's Day."

And the punchline is: "Hey, your kid and my kid are beating up our kid."

*or:*

The one about the John Wayne toilet paper.

Lester Paul used to swim across the Peace River. This was back in Fort Vermilion, and most of us were impressed by his athletic ability. He would go down the riverbank early every morning in the summer and swim out to the island in the centre of the river, get out and shake himself off, then walk across the island and disappear. None of us had ever seen him swim to the other shore and then back, but we were willing to take his word for it. Nobody asked him why he was doing it; we figured it was just because he could. Or because he was bored. One time, though, one of the new teachers From Out caught him coming back up the bank after his return trip and asked him why he was swimming. "I'm in training for the Olympics," Lester said, and then he kept on walking.

It was only a few days before every person From Out was talking about Lester Paul and debating his potential to make the national swim team. Most of them seemed to think he had very little chance for success. Some thought he might make the team, but wouldn't finish in the medals. Only a few of them dismissed the whole thing as a joke, which it was, though Lester *was* doing something remarkable with all that swimming. It was a perfect example of what White People do when they encounter Aboriginal humour. They take it the wrong way. That is, they take it way too serious.

Every so often some graduate student in Cultural Anthropology would show up in Fort Vermilion looking to do some research. These students were easily recognized by their complete lack of irony (not to mention beards and knapsacks) and it was considered sport to send them back to the city with notebooks full of falsehoods. It was the same way the Samoans had treated Margaret Mead. "Coming of age in Samoa? Jeez, we were just kidding." Only in the Fort it would be "Take a joke, eh?"

My sister Darla was once cornered by a fervently sincere woman who wanted to learn about, you guessed it, the Native Experience. This happens to Darla a lot, actually. She's never been able to figure out why. But she's relentlessly polite, and maybe that's why people feel they can talk to her; she brings it on herself. This particular woman was fascinated by sweat lodges and was asking my sister all sorts of questions about the rituals involved. Now the Bush Cree don't know from sweat lodges. Not part of the culture. No totem poles, either. Darla gently tried to explain this to the woman, but all that did was get the woman flustered and apologetic. This is an illustration of another thing White People do to Indians. They act as if there is one homogenous Aboriginal culture. As if all members of the First Nations share the same exact history and mythology.

They don't. Hell, even the jokes are different from area to area. Here's an example of how an eternal question would finally be answered. With slightly different tribal interpretations.

"Why did the chicken cross the road?"
MI'KMAQ: "He was on his way to Burnt Church."
MOHAWK: "To put up a blockade."

OJIBWAY: "That is the chicken's inherent right."

SALISH: "It was going upstream to spawn."

CREE: "Was the chicken running away from residential
school?"

INUIT: "What road?"

SLAVEE: "What's a chicken?"

Of course any member of a band or tribal council would probably want to punish the chicken for crossing the road without permission. The chicken's entire family could lose their jobs. Anybody working for the Department of Native and Northern Affairs would assume the chicken was en route to fill out form W11867-643, which pertains to indigenous poultry and its transportation and distribution. Me, I think the answer is "I'll take a bucket of chicken, extra-crispy, with some fries and coleslaw." Oh, and a side of gravy.

My sister was once asked, by a different but equally well-intentioned White Person, the other eternal question: "What do you people want?" The question was rather vague; it could have meant what do you women want or what do you parents want or what do you prison guards want or what do you volleyball players want or any number of other things that are part of Darla's identity. Could even have been about bingo. My sister took a wild guess, however, and figured this particular White Person was really asking, "What do you Indians want?" Darla happened to have the perfect answer.

"What we want," she said, "is for you people to lighten up."

All together now:

*These two Indians walk into a bar... You'd think one of them would've ducked.*

# BUFFALO TALES
# AND ACADEMIC TRAILS

........................

{ KAREN FROMAN }

*W*HEN I looked up one day and found myself to be a twenty-seven-year-old divorced mother of two with a grade nine education, it was an "Oh crap, I'd better get off my butt and go back to school" moment. Trouble was, I had no idea what to do with myself at university. So I entered the University of Manitoba through the Access Program. On orientation day I stepped into a classroom full of Native students who were all staring at this strange pale woman in the doorway. Yes, I am a pigmentally challenged Native person. (I can't really blame it on my mom, either, since she is the brownest white woman I've ever met. But I digress.) My initial introduction to university was a bit daunting, to say the least. I faced challenges to my identity, my degree of Nativeness and my right to be a part of both the Access Program and the Aboriginal Students Association. Native people of mixed ancestry are all too familiar with this reaction on the part of our darker sisters and brothers.

Fortunately, I soon encountered not only some fantastic professors but also an amusing and sagacious book that gave me a way to resist the "not Native enough" nonsense. First, the professors.

Believe it or not, a Native Studies class can be a pretty damn funny place, despite the often depressing subject matter. When you have a professor who is willing to stand up in front of a classroom of 150 students and pretend to be a buffalo by hooking his hands like horns beside his head, you know you are in for a good class. Dr. Fred Shore has the ability to make topics like the Indian Act interesting and amusing by pointing out, with a sharp, sometimes sarcastic wit, the many contradictions in government policy and action. In his introductory course, we learned about Aboriginal resistance to government control both through academic readings and through personal storytelling. Another one of my professors, Dr. Chris Trott, who teaches Inuit Studies, took the humorous route one day when explaining the differences that can exist in dialect. He used marriage vows as an example. The northern Baffin Island Inuktitut version of "Will you take this woman to be your wedded wife?" translates as "will you take this woman and have sex with her like an animal?" in the southern Baffin Island dialect. This cracked most of us right up, though a few students were rather shocked. It was an effective way of getting across the fact that Native languages and cultures vary greatly, even within a "single" culture.

I think I admired the humorous aspect of their teaching so much because I had always used humour as a way of defending myself. I did not fit into any preconceived notion of either "Native" or "White." With strangers, I often remained silent or reacted with hostility. I reacted most negatively to comments from other Native people, which hurt more than the same comments coming from non-Native people would have. But I wasn't far into my first year of university when I stumbled across a book that not only made me fall on the floor laughing but gave me the tools to be okay with who I was and what I looked like. Drew Hayden Taylor's *Funny, You Don't Look Like One: Observations from a Blue-Eyed Ojibway* caught my eye one day in the campus bookstore.[1] As a green-eyed Mohawk, if I had a nickel for every time I have heard that remark myself, I'd be a bloody millionaire. (To hell with Lotto 6/49: the next time someone says that to me, I'll charge them a loonie!) Taylor's book, and the rest of his *Funny* series that followed, let me know I was not the only one. They also gave me some funny material about being a pasty-white Indian to add to my repertoire.

Now, as I forge my own teaching career in Native Studies, I draw upon these amusing teachers and authors like Taylor for inspiration and guidance. Humour in the classroom can promote healing and unity. Witty personal storytelling and published commentaries help tie academic texts to the day-to-day reality of contemporary Native life. Shared laughter in the face of painful experiences can serve to bridge the divide, real or imagined, between Aboriginal and non-Aboriginal students as well.

My own sense of humour is rather dark; I tend towards what is commonly referred to as "survivor humour," and as such a person I am a bit on the sarcastic side. Humour, in the Native context, is a coping mechanism; we use it to deal with five hundred years of colonization and to help non-Native people understand us. And comedy in the classroom can relieve the tension for everybody. I am a physical person, and I tend to use body language and facial expressions to convey humour. For example, when I teach students about the 1969 "White Paper" and its contemporary counterpart, the First Nations Governance Act (FNGA), I refer to the White Paper as "the thing that wouldn't die," speaking in a horror-movie type of voice and widening my eyes: "It came from Ottawa, oozing its way out of the muck known as Parliament Hill. It was 1969, and Jean Chrétien, the Minister of Indian Affairs, had a plan to solve the 'Indian

Problem' once and for all." When I get to the FNGA, I say something like, "We thought the White Paper had died a miserable death on some Liberal shelf, but it lived on in various guises, lulling us into complacency, only to re-emerge from the ooze. Like dirty laundry, it never goes away." In the classroom, I also rely quite heavily on material from well-known Native comics, such as Don Burnstick's "You know you're a redskin if..." routines and Charlie Hill's now classic story, "He said, 'Why don't you people go back where you came from? So I camped in his backyard," to get my point across.

The focus of my research and teaching is contemporary Native culture and identity in large urban areas. I spend a lot of time talking about stereotypes, myths and racism, all of which must be dealt with in a classroom of students from diverse backgrounds. Not all students in a Native Studies class are Native, nor have those who are Native necessarily grown up on a reserve or learned anything about their respective cultures. Both Native and non-Native students have preconceived notions of what a Native person acts and looks like, too, and I ain't it. Few people expect to see someone as pale as I am in front of the class announcing *"She'kon, skennonkowa?"* which essentially means "Hi, how are you?" in Mohawk. Since I teach in Manitoba, where people are more familiar with the Métis, the Ojibway and the Cree, being Mohawk makes me even more of an oddball, and it gives me an edge in teaching Native Studies from a broad perspective. Many students are surprised by some of the issues I raise in class and the manner in which I raise them.

For example, when I am preparing for a classroom discussion on intermarriage and its impact on culture and identity for Native people, I assign students Bonita Lawrence's examination of the experiences of contemporary urban Natives in Toronto. Lawrence's study covers a number of issues, such as the anxiety that can be felt over whether or not a particular individual is "Indian enough." Lawrence raises the important point that, in a way, even to discuss "mixed-race urban Native identity" is to fall into the trap of "weighing and measuring 'Indianness' to see how well we fit."[2] Rather than recognizing that the categories of "status" and "non-status" "were created by the settler government to divide us," we act as if these divisions have always existed.[3] However, I take issue with Lawrence's conclusion regarding physical appearance. She states that most of the individuals she interviewed "did not have much sense of the extent of the daily privilege they enjoyed from having white skin. Their concerns about not fitting in within the Native community at times appeared to overshadow their awareness of the fact that their lives were made much easier by virtue of *not* looking Native."[4] Lawrence does acknowledge that unless such divisions over physical appearance are addressed in a respectful manner, "the different circumstances that white-looking and dark Native people face will continue to be unspoken."[5] Yet she does not directly confront the complex spectre of internal racism that this attitude implies.

To counterbalance this academic work, I assign it along with Drew Hayden Taylor's articles "Half Empty or Half Full?" and "How Native Is Native if You're Native?"[6] Taylor tackles the issue squarely, and in a humorous manner. He reminds us that, in the past, "the lighter skinned Native people were more acceptable in the mainstream... but today, with the advent of political correctness, the reverse is becoming the norm. The darker you are, the more acceptable you are."[7] In addition, Taylor says, a dark-haired Native person does not have to face "the reverse preconceptions people like [me] must deal with."[8] He ends by commenting that if life really was that much simpler for "white-looking" Natives, he would not have to write articles like this.

The discussion generated by Lawrence and Taylor's works can sometimes be far more animated than I have anticipated. One particular class I assigned these articles to was almost entirely female and evenly split between "urban" and "reserve" students, most of them obviously Native in appearance. The majority of them had either never thought about these issues or had bought into the stereotypes. In other words, "pale" Native people were not seen as Native by my "darker" students. Most of the students simply assumed that the "pale" students, including myself, were white. When I asked students if they would deny themselves love, or a friend or a family member love, based simply on the colour of another person's skin, most seemed surprised by the question and could not immediately answer. Many eventually decided that it was a better choice to marry "within the gene pool," based primarily on retaining "Indian status." In the end, though, most could also see the point I was trying to make: that, pale or dark, we can and should keep our identities and cultures as Native peoples. By using Taylor's articles and employing a sense of humour about my own appearance, I managed to keep our discussion of a potentially volatile topic respectful and lively.

My attempts at humour in the classroom are not always successful, of course. And it is often my Native students who laugh, at least at first, while my non-Native students look at me as if I have tulips growing out of my head. Non-Native students can have trouble grasping what is funny about something, and they seem shocked when their Native classmates and I laugh at touchy topics. I explain that, for us, being able to laugh is a way of coping.

Over the years, I have amassed an impressive collection of comic strips that address Native issues. One of my favourites is a *Bizarro* that shows two southwestern "generic Plains" guys looking at smoke signals from across a valley. One guy is telling the other, "It says Aieeey! Godzilla!" and in the distance you can see a tiny Godzilla beside a tiny village of tepees. This comic is a good jumping-off point for classroom discussions of cultural appropriation, the "Hollywood Indian" stereotype and the whole question of what makes us laugh and why. Another strip in my collection is from *Family Circus*. It shows two little boys, one dressed as a cowboy and the other as a businessman. The one in the business suit is saying, "And I'll be an Indian... with a casino." Again, this generates laughs, but it also opens the way to looking at stereotypes about Native people and gambling and to discussing the pros and cons of economic development. Interestingly, most of my non-Native students tend to take such cartoons as reflections of reality and so do not see the different levels of humour in them at first.

I also use toys to demonstrate that stereotypes of Aboriginal people are alive and well. I started with a small plastic Snoopy dressed in Navajo-style clothes, holding his hand up as if to say "How." I have always wanted some toys from the Playmobil "Native American Indian/Wild West" line, and I recently found an inexpensive store in Toronto that had several of the sets. I picked up two, as they are fantastically and comically inaccurate. The series supposedly depicts the Plains Indian, complete with face paint, feathered war bonnets, spears and knives. One figure of a Native male came with a feathered spear, a war bonnet and *five* knives! Another item I picked up was a "Native bendy pen" (it is actually called this), which I found at an airport in a bucket advertising "authentic" Canadian souvenirs (it was made in Taiwan). The pen depicts the generic Plains-style Native in "traditional" dress complete with a feathered bonnet made of flexible foam. The figure is attached to the pen by a maple leaf. (And the pen doesn't work, either!) The stereotypes depicted in the toys are so blatant that they often shock students into thinking outside of their own cultural comfort zones and questioning their own belief systems.

Canadian mainstream education historically presented history from the Euro-Canadian viewpoint. As J.M. Blaut asserts

in *The Colonizer's Model of the World*, "Textbooks are an important window to a culture; more than just books, they are semi-
official statements of exactly what the opinion-forming elite of
the culture want the educated youth of that culture to believe to
be true about the past and present world."[9] Many Native people
have begun to talk about their experiences in school, about how
we were taught to hate ourselves and to feel shame over our "savage" ancestors, who had the audacity to defend themselves and
their land from the "gift" of European "civilization"[10] As Emma
LaRocque writes, the prevalent image of "the lurking, crouching,
tomahawk swinging, scalp taking, painted, naked howling savage (who was rumoured to be my forefather) had a profound and
lasting impact on me and others"[11]

Personally, I had experiences of being told to "go back to the
reserve" and of being called a "dirty halfbreed squaw"; I was
also told that, as a Native person, I was doomed to educational
failure. Although the education system, at least in Manitoba, is
undergoing changes that address this kind of stereotyping and
now attempts to teach Native history and culture from a Native
perspective, these images and ideas are still with us. The vast
majority of teachers currently employed in the public school system have no training in Native Studies, and fall back on the stereotypes and the old methods of teaching. Aboriginal people are
still museum pieces. Our children are still making paper tepees
and paper-plate dreamcatchers in school and being told that
this is Native culture.

In an effort to counter such teaching, I have been a parent vol-
unteer at my own children's elementary school for several years.
The school has a predominantly non-Native student body, and
most of the students know me as "the funny lady who teaches us
Native Studies," not as Hayley and Logan's mom. Working with
elementary-school children is a lot of fun, as little kids are very
open to new ideas, particularly if the person teaching them is

willing to leap around the classroom pretending to be a buffalo. If you are willing to be goofy, the kids will learn more. I teach in a way that corrects the "generic Indian" idea and shows kids that Native people today are doctors, lawyers, teachers and nurses. Even though Native people today eat at McDonald's and watch cable TV, I tell them, many of us still maintain our cultures and beliefs. When I ask a class to draw a picture of what they think a Native person looks like, I inevitably end up with twenty drawings of a person in braids and buckskins next to a tepee. Then I will ask them to look at me, and I say, "Am I a Native person?" Most kids get it right away. I am also very hands-on in my work with young children, bringing in my hand drum, hides, scrapers, bones and powwow music. I get the biggest laughs when I give my lessons on the Arctic, as I bring in several sealskins and ask the kids how the Inuit make the skins soft. Most of them have no idea, and when I start to chew on the skins I get the "Ewwww" reaction, accompanied by a lot of giggles. There is always at least one child willing to try it, since the "ick factor" works well in teaching young people, particularly little boys.

Here's something that happened to me about two years ago at my favourite coffee shop. I had gone in for my usual late-afternoon latte and was chatting with the barista, who suddenly said, "You're Native, right?" I replied in the affirmative. He proceeded to tell me that he was reading a book written by a Blackfoot person. Since part of it was written in Blackfoot, he wanted to know if I could translate it for him. I laughed and said no, that I am Mohawk, not Blackfoot, and cannot even read my own language. He appeared puzzled, then disappointed. "Oh, well, I was hoping you could, because I don't understand the language and I feel left out." I laughed again. "Well, now you know how it feels, eh?" I said. His jaw just about hit the floor before he realized how ridiculous his assumptions had been, and he too started to laugh. This story always generates a few chuckles in class, and it brings out similar stories from students, a sharing that I encourage. If we can learn to laugh not only at ourselves but at the absurd assumptions and stereotypes regarding Native peoples, then we have made the first steps towards a world that treats all people with true respect and honour.

— NOTES —

1. Drew Hayden Taylor, *Funny, You Don't Look Like One: Observations from a Blue-Eyed Ojibway*. Penticton: Theytus Books, 1996.

2. Bonita Lawrence, "Mixed-Race Urban Native People: Surviving a Legacy of Policies of Genocide." In *Expressions in Canadian Native Studies*, eds. R.F. Laliberte et al. Saskatoon: University of Saskatchewan Extension Press, 2000, p. 82.

3. Bonita Lawrence, "Mixed-Race Urban Native People: Surviving a Legacy of Policies of Genocide," p. 76.

4. Bonita Lawrence, "Mixed-Race Urban Native People: Surviving a Legacy of Policies of Genocide," pp. 85–86.

5. Bonita Lawrence, "Mixed-Race Urban Native People: Surviving a Legacy of Policies of Genocide," p. 86.

6. Drew Hayden Taylor's "Half Empty or Half Full?" appears in *Furious Observations of a Blue-Eyed Ojibway: Funny, You Don't Look Like One Three*. Penticton: Theytus Books, 2002. "How Native Is Native if You're Native?" appears in *Further Adventures of a Blue-Eyed Ojibway: Funny, You Don't Look Like One Two*. Penticton: Theytus Books, 1999.

7. Drew Hayden Taylor, "Half Empty or Half Full?" pp. 103–4.

8. Drew Hayden Taylor, "Half Empty or Half Full?" p. 106.

9. J.M. Blaut, *The Colonizer's Model of the World: Geographical Diffusionism and Eurocentric History*. New York, London: Guilford Press, 1993, p. 6.

10. Emma LaRocque, *Native Writers Resisting Colonizing Practices in Canadian Historiography and Literature*. Dissertation. Winnipeg: University of Manitoba, 1999. Pp. 181–87.

11. Emma LaRocque, *Native Writers Resisting Colonizing Practices in Canadian Historiography and Literature*, p. 187.

*Astutely* selected ETHNO-BASED
examples of CULTURAL *jocularity* and
*racial* COMICALNESS

. . . . . . . .

{ EXAMPLES 10, 11, 12, 13, 14 AND 15 }

Q: *What do you get when you have fifty lesbians together with fifty band-office workers?*
A: *You get a hundred people who don't do dick.*

Q: *What did the Indian wearing the suit say?*
A: *"Not guilty."*

Q: *Did you hear about the Native guy who moved out east?*
A: *Yeah, he heard there was no work out there.*

Q: *What do you get when you cross a Haida with an Ojibway?*
A: *A Haida-way.*

Q: *What do you get when you cross somebody who's French with somebody who's Cherokee?*
A: *Somebody who's Fre-kee.*

Q: *What's the definition of Native foreplay?*
A: *"Hey, you awake?"*

{ EXAMPLE 16 }

THE ABORIGINAL PEOPLES *of Canada want to have National Aboriginal Day recognized as a national holiday. All Aboriginal people would get the whole day off—except for the Métis, who would only get half a day off.*

{ EXAMPLE 17 }

WHEN NASA WAS *preparing for the Apollo Project, it took the astronauts to a Navajo reservation in Arizona for training. One day, a Navajo elder and his son came across the space crew walking among the rocks. The elder, who spoke only Navajo, asked a question. His son translated for the NASA people: "What are these guys in the big suits doing?" One of the astronauts said that they were practising for a trip to the moon.*

*When his son relayed this comment, the Navajo elder got all excited and asked if it would be possible to give the astronauts a message to deliver to the moon. Recognizing a promotional opportunity when he saw one, a NASA official accompanying the astronauts said, "Why certainly!" and told an underling to get a tape recorder. The Navajo elder's comments into the microphone were brief. The NASA official asked the son if he would translate what his father had said. The son listened to the recording and laughed uproariously. But he refused to translate.*

*So the NASA people took the tape to a nearby Navajo village and played it for other members of the tribe. They too laughed long and loudly but refused to translate the elder's message to the moon.*

*Finally, an official government translator was summoned. After he eventually stopped laughing, the translator relayed the message: "Watch out for these assholes—they have come to steal your land."*

# RUBY LIPS

. . . . . . . . . . . . .

{ LOUISE PROFEIT-LEBLANC }

*H*ANGING UP the phone, in my office on the twelfth floor of a high-rise building in the nation's capital, I laughed out loud, causing my assistant to give me a look of "What now?" It had been three years since I pulled up roots from my home in the North and ventured forth to work in the city on behalf of Aboriginal artists across Canada. In my former life, as Native Heritage Advisor for the Yukon government, I had the opportunity to meet many wonderful and interesting people, particularly elders, storytellers and others whose life stories were definitely worth telling. My artistic practice as a storyteller was on hold, and only on special occasions was there the chance to share stories of my people in the Yukon. But then I was asked by the Trickster, still alive and well in the guise of Drew Hayden Taylor, to write down one of my stories. A broad grin settled on my face.

I already knew the story I was going to tell. It was one that I had on occasion told friends, about my hero and heroine couple: Johnny Silverfox and his lifelong partner, Mary Malcom, affectionately known as Johnny Six Toes (or Johnny Fock [Fox], as his wife called him) and Maryjowah by the townspeople in Mayo, where I spent my childhood years. How does a place that is the homeland of the Nacho N'yak Dun First Nation get a name like Mayo? This is part of the comedy that First Nations people across this land know all too well. Mayo is not short for mayonnaise. It is short for George Mayo, an Italian prospector who was hungry in his search for silver in the creeks and tributaries of the Stewart River—the river where my people had dipped their buckets and cast their lines for fish since the time before time. Of course George had his own experience with the colonizers; his real name was Georgio.

It is important that I provide an orientation for you, the reader, to prepare you for this little journey to another world. It is a world where many of the simple things in life are so horrendous that the only way to stay sane is to simply laugh about it all. The journey is a story from my own life, plucked out of the air as it flew from the surface of my childhood memory to be trapped in the web of the written word and carefully placed on the page. Stories like this one are meant to be told, spoken, shared with a listener, with many nuances, sound effects and cadences of language and much pointing of the mouth, the chin and the nose. Expulsions of air to demonstrate a strength, a sorrow, a shock. Eye and body movements that resemble each of the characters playing out their parts, hand and arm gestures, giving, taking, the head tilting, dropping, weaving from side to side. The simple wrinkling of the forehead and the random expression of emotions—all these faces of the one storyteller bring each scene of the story to life. Ahhh! and so much can be said with pauses and pure silence. But You, deprived reader, will have to envision the story for yourself, depend on your mind's eye to see the theatrical elements.

It is important to realize that this story is told in honour of its main characters. It is without prejudice, judgement, blame or ridicule. These characters have been chosen as my subjects to present a sampling of Aboriginal humour. Humour in this context is a teaching, a life lesson. It should not be confused with the slapstick stand-up comedy that many Aboriginal comedians are good at. The kind of humour this story contains is really not so funny when you get right down to it, but it thrives among the poorest of our populations. It stems from those whose lives are a constant struggle, full of the strife and extreme hardship associated with poverty. This type of humour shows the true resilience of people who can look at life's tests and laugh at them. This adaptability results in a lifting of their own spirits and the spirits of those around them. "Happy-makers" is what our elders call these people. They are every bit as important as the successful hunters and fishermen; they could even *be* successful hunters and fishermen.

So many things have been taken from Aboriginal peoples, but our sense of humour has remained intact. It has provided us with solace, a healthy escape, and a way to learn both acceptance of and detachment from what life dishes out. This story is a reminder to all of us who have been there, who might have forgotten how to laugh now that our lives are easier. For all of my people who are still suffering from poverty, poor housing, disease, addictions, sorrow, loss and illiteracy, and who have no means to improve their lives, I offer this story as a payment, in gratitude for the many lessons I've learned during my lifetime from all of you.

. . . . . . . . .

WHEN WE WERE CHILDREN, every day of summer held a promise of adventure. In the dusty long hot hours of continuous daylight, we would constantly cruise around on our bikes waiting for something exciting to happen. And most times it did. In our little village, Main Street and the Stewart River ran perpendicular to each other, which made surveillance easy from either the road or the dike built up on the riverbank to protect us from spring floods. Life was good. With so much daylight and so much freedom, the village seemed always to be in rehearsal, preparing another scene for us to enjoy. Some days we would saunter down to the docks and watch the float planes get loaded up with supplies. Huge fuel drums were rolled up the ramps into the aircrafts' tails. We'd stand gawking as the pilots changed their oil right there in the river, appreciating the colourful swirls of oil slicks on the water. Occasionally a sucker fish might come and suck at the foam lapping up on the shore. The sucking noises were gross, since we knew that the fish were actually sucking near a pipe that dumped raw sewage into the river.

Further upriver some of the village fishermen would be loading up their flat-bottom river boats. Their impatient dogs would be yelping to get in the boats and get on with the task at hand, looking forward to the eventual full belly of fish. Being curious about the goings-on of young lovers, we would occasionally sneak up on a couple walking down the dike, wondering what the guy was whispering in the girl's ear that made her giggle. Once we saw a couple take a trip across the Stewart River in a new canvas canoe, dock on the opposite shore and then go into the bushes to enjoy a bit of privacy among the fluttering sounds of poplar leaves. We joked that they might even do "it" over there. Ohhh, the corrupt minds of summer bikers. We were the watchers, the watch guards, the voyeurs of our town, making everybody's business our own.

Funny how summer brought out both the best and the worst in people. Every summer someone would threaten to shoot another person's dog for getting into the pen of a protected bitch or raiding a meat cache. Either charge was an immediate death warrant. The loud shouting matches would beckon us, but the swearing usually resulted in the slamming of doors, the yelping of dogs being locked in the porch and eventual forgiveness by both parties. We'd park our bikes out of harm's way to watch foolish young men driving their pickup trucks like maniacs, tearing up the gravel roads, leaving the girls they were trying to impress coughing in a cloud of dust. But the main event was always on Main Street. This was the popular locale. This was the place where the street theatre in our village really took place.

So picture this. On this main street were the Silver Inn Cafe & Beer Parlour and the Chateau Mayo Cafe & Bar, exotic names left over from a previous era, the silver rush at Keno Hill mines. On the corner by the Chateau Mayo Hotel was the CP Air ticket office, as well as the post office, which had more general deliveries than box addresses. Across the street was Danny's store and farther down Main was Graham's. These stores, in stiff competition with each other, both sold rotting fruit and vegetables and mouldy bread at exorbitant prices. People who didn't have cars would be at their mercy, not able to drive south to the capital city for supplies selling at half the cost. All these places were close together, handy for any Main Street action. There would always be a guaranteed audience of grocery shoppers or those who were picking up their mail. The centre of the action was usually the bar—or the post office, which became popular on family allowance and pogey days.

On one corner of Main, perpendicular to the street that ran straight up towards the hospital and police station, was the infamous "sewer box." Painted hunter green and built out of plywood, this box covered the pump for the town's main sewer line. The box was perfectly harmless, but it was useful as a seat on which the elders would often be resting or as a gathering place around which the elders would stand, telling stories, sharing gossip or patiently waiting for something to happen like the rest of us. This sewer box sits there to this day, and if it could speak it would have many, many crazy stories to tell.

At the other end of Main Street, the other end of town, lived Johnny Six Toes and his partner, Maryjowah, with their children. They also had a dog who lived in their basement and was perpetually pregnant with another litter of puppies. For years Johnny and Maryjowah had lived in a rundown log house, but after having two children later in life, they were given a band house with running water and an electric stove. When Indian Affairs finally decided to get into the twentieth century and provide Indian homes with all the necessary amenities, it was hell on those who were used to a wood stove for heat and cooking. A lot of food was burnt and thrown out as a result. Eventually people got used to this new invention and learned to take their kettle off the stove when they left the house. They also discovered that if they ran out of fuel they could turn on the oven, and this would provide them with enough heat to heat the entire upstairs.

The day in question was not unlike any other day. The children got up and wanted some breakfast, but there was no bread. Maryjowah had asked Johnny to go and buy a loaf of bread from Danny's store. She had given him all her money, which in total was about two dollars. This errand was suggested at approximately ten that morning. Johnny had taken his sweet time to get up. With the aches and pains of a poisoned liver, it was hard to get going in the morning. Maryjowah had watched Johnny waddle down the street but since then hadn't seen hide nor hair of him. The children had gone out to play with their bellies empty. When we kids saw Maryjowah heading down the street towards the Chateau Mayo, we knew full well that she was spitting mad. She was hostile, and the first dog that came around her got clubbed with a stick she'd kept handy for just that purpose.

"Git outta heah! Git! Go on!" The dog took off shocked, yelping from the impact of her weapon across its back. Maryjowah's eyes were black with anger. She was mumbling and swearing under her breath.

"Ya kids see Johnny Fock? Where 'n the heow is he? God dang son a bit!"

We laughed and went on ahead of her to find him sitting on the "speaker's box," weaving back and forth, inebriated now after drinking up the bread money. His shirt was tight around his enormous belly, which hung over pants held up with a piece of string. He was a sight to behold, and a smelly one at that. His body reeked. Personal hygiene was not on Johnny's list of priorities, and on that summer day beads of sweat were pouring down his forehead and dripping off the end of his nose. His greasy, thick hair was sticking up all over his head. But most amazing was this wild thing going on with his eyes. In his drunken state, Johnny was totally incapable of controlling them. His eyes kept crossing or rolling upwards under his eyelids, so that only the whites of his eyeballs showed. Weird! This was so funny to us. Johnny tried to joke with us about it, but he made little progress in the "straight-eye" department. His head was shaking from side to side, and he was mumbling under his breath as he pushed the bulk of his body up to a more comfortable position on the box. We felt kind of sorry for him. He was definitely suffering from the heat. His feet were swollen right up from his "diabeetee." "Yah, yah, that the one he make my feet fat, that diabeetee."

Johnny had explained to us kids that because of his diabetes, Ski-Doo boot liners were the only things that he could wear on his feet. We would watch him as he carefully manoeuvred his way across gravel patches on the road to avoid sharp rocks that might hurt his aching feet. He lumbered a little easier in the grass or on sidewalks with these makeshift shoes. His feet must have been cooking. The temperatures shot up to nearly eighty degrees that summer. Even the insistent mosquitoes found shelter under leaves and grasses to avoid the intense heat. Grasshoppers' legs creaked as they jumped into little clouds of dust along the roadside. Dogs sought shade in their doghouses or under trees, their water dishes needing to be filled up constantly. It is on days like this that the elders' saying "Hot like a dog" makes total sense. Dogs around the village sat with their tongues hanging out, panting, trying to cool down, blinking the dust out of their eyes and snapping at the occasional sandfly that had dared to venture out into the heat. Even the river seemed to run slower in this extreme temperature. The bush was like tinder making crunchy sounds under our bike tires. There was an imminent feeling in the air that the seasonal forest fires were just waiting to happen. There was a heating up in all aspects of life in the village, including Johnny Six Toes's wife's temper. Now she was hot!

"How ya know she mad? You speak true now, ya kids? Is that right my Maryjowah is coming down to get me? Hoh! I in dawg house now. I not scared. You gonna see, it gonna be okay. Maybe!" Johnny hit his big belly. "She like it, you know?"

Once Johnny Fox had made us kids laugh so hard by trying to convince us that he was pregnant. What other conclusion could a man who didn't understand what was happening to his diseased liver, swollen with cirrhosis, have come to?

"Whatcha think, you kid? You think I gonna get baby? Pretty soon, I think I gonna be first man to get baby! What you think?" At this comment he had tipped slightly backwards and let out the biggest belly laugh. As he explained his dilemma to us, there were a few moments when we thought it might just be true. We even fantasized his becoming very famous about it all. You know the headlines: "First Man to Have Baby Hails from Yukon!" Johnny Six Toes was hilarious, and we could tell that he found it amusing to keep us all guessing.

"An' you see heah? This where my finger he use to be, when I'm kid. Doctor he cut it off that tine. Try to make it shorter winter I guess, just like that beaver he chew off his own toe to make winter short. That's da one, same kind. Howcum it stay cold just the same?" Johnny knew the old stories of his people and had previously related this one to us. The legend was about how Beaver and Porcupine had determined the length of the seasons by Beaver chewing off one of his toes. From that point on, I dubbed Johnny Fox "Beaver Man."

Johnny Silverfox was named appropriately. Not because he moved like a beautiful silver fox across the landscape, no, but because he was as tricky as a fox. He was truly foxy, especially when he needed money for beer. I would witness his prowess later on in my life when I spotted him coming into the bar. Coming in for the hunt. In for the kill! It was only a matter of minutes after adjusting his failing eyes to the darkness of the barroom before he had figured out the strangers in the house and made a beeline to sit immediately next to one of them. These were men on summer work crews, pilots, geologists, miners or guys working construction who were in for an evening beer, a cool one. Johnny would catch them off guard by sidling right up to them and letting them in on a few pointers about whose land they were working on.

"We gif it all up that land, you know? We getta hard time, but we don't care. You know when I'm kid, I getta a hard time. I born with six toes you know. Six fingers too. You believe it?" The unsuspecting visitor had now been drawn into compassionate mode for this dishevelled and unwashed friend parked next to him.

"Gee I dry!" Johnny would say, clearing his throat. He had had a severe headache all morning and now needed a cool one too. "You know what? I got six toe. You know that? Got six toe on both foot. You believe it? Use to be six finger on my hand."

Holding up his hands, Johnny would explain how the doctor had cut off his extra finger so that the other children wouldn't tease him. The pilot or miner nodded his head in disbelief as he viewed the little stump on each of Johnny's large brown paws.

"You wannna see my toe, six toe? You gonna see it? You gif me five buck, I gonna show you. You wanna see it, hey?" Johnny would clumsily try to get down off the high stool to take off his boot liners.

Immediately the pilot went for his wallet and quickly gave Johnny some money.

"I believe you. I'll give you five bucks *not* to take them off. Okay?" Johnny would thank him and saunter victoriously to the end of the bar, where he ordered beer for take out.

The barmaid would give Johnny Six Toes his three beers in a brown paper bag and send him on his way. Another score for the Fox! On his way out he'd wave to the unsuspecting, who had also lined up at the bar, as if they were all his long lost friends. They were none the wiser.

"Hunting was good today," Johnny would think to himself. "Pretty good, not too shabby!"

When Maryjowah was drunk or mad, she was extremely difficult to understand. Her screeching, high-pitched voice, delivering words at rapid fire in an incomprehensible, mostly northern Tutchone, was definitely a challenge to decipher. On family allowance day in Mayo many of us lower-income mothers were eager to get our cheques at the post office, an appreciated supplement to our monthly income, to buy extras for our children. Maryjowah was no different. But her partying the night before, on some home brew at her friend's place, would make the trip to the post office a bit treacherous. Her bandy legs turned to rubber and caused her to stumble and fall where there were no obstacles in her way. Sometimes she would call out to bystanders to help her up.

"J'eye. My leg he gif up on me. Help me up, you fellas!" Until someone answered her call of distress, she would lie back in the willows giggling to herself about her predicament.

Finally, with much effort and determination, Maryjowah

would reach her destination. By the time I arrived on the scene she was often screaming out unintelligible cuss words at the postmistress, who was looking disgusted and was about to close the window against the stream of profanities flying her way. The postmistress did hold the power and could make the decision not to give a family allowance cheque to a drunken mother.

"Ya getcha mat chess cheque yet?" Maryjowah screeched out at me.

"What? I'm sorry, I don't know what you are saying."

"You, ya getcha mat chess cheque yet?"

Maryjowah watched me as I opened my post-office box and pulled out the beloved government cheque. She fired another dirty look at the postmistress.

"Got dang son a bit! She no give me my mat chess cheque. Wha 'n heow? Howcum you got your cheque. She no give it to me. Rotten son a gun! She tell me, I too drunk. Tell her I not drunk. Go 'head! Abee ow! Damn shit!" And with that last comment Maryjowah stumbled over towards the exit, slung open the door and slammed out without her precious "mattress cheque."

Now, like a stormy dust devil, Maryjowah was making her way down the street. The village dogs were clearing out of the way. Her eyes darted back and forth and up ahead. In the heat of her anger, she was not about to expose her condition to any snoopy onlooker, and she avoided people on the sidewalk by ducking into the bushes along the road as she made her way to Main Street. Peeking out now, she began to holler loudly at the giant of a man she called her husband.

"Johnny Fock! You make me mad 'n hell, Johnny Fock. You got dat bread? I send you down long tines ago. What'n heow? Now look you, you got all juice up. God dang son a bit! Jus feel like to club you down!"

Johnny was smiling and using his tongue to push back a little plug of tobacco into his lower lip. The brown tobacco juice was slobbering down his chin. His tongue darted in and out, catching a few straggler chunks of tobacco. He patted the top of the Copenhagen tin and placed it slowly back into his pocket. He was ready now for the final act, the verbal blows of his wife's attack. The twinkle in his eyes should have been a warning to us as he pushed himself into a ready position on the box.

Shaking his head, trying his best to focus on the little fireball to his left, he broke into a little grin and then, looking directly at Maryjowah, burst into song, to the tune of the old Hank Williams hit "Your Cheatin' Heart." In the most romantic posturing that he could muster up, Johnny began his cooing melody.

"Who gonna kiss my ruby lips? Who gonna kiss my ruby lips?" Smacking in between these two lines, Johnny Fox comes up to the final crescendo. He has conspired with the gods and is aiming to take the heat of his woman's anger. He keeps repeating the same two lines and watching for the reaction from Maryjowah. A sign of weakening, perhaps? Yes! It is happening! Maryjowah's eyes dart around her, making sure there is no other competition. Her heart has melted within her. All is forgiven. The past is the past, there is no other for her, but she must put up a little resistance to keep her own sense of dignity and pride. She shouts back in a teasing manner.

"Not me, that for shore!" Her little smile indicates that she is flattered. She likes his serenading. As Johnny continues the replay of the same words, giving them all the twang he can, she slides in closer until she is sitting right beside him. Aha! Johnny Fox has scored. He has dissipated the heat and vengeance that only an angered woman can hold. He has successfully and artistically found a means to resolve his personal conflict and has won back the heart of his lady.

"Whazat you got in your pocket?" Maryjowah says, pointing to a bulging beer stuffed into Johnny's shirt sleeve.

"Thas a bee-air. Das Shra. You wan sum?"

Looking up sweetly into his eyes now, Maryjowah locks her arm into his, lifting him up with all hundred pounds of her own strength. They begin the long walk home, slowing down for an occasional belting out of Johnny's love song for Maryjowah.

"Save tha' wun for home. For afta, you hear?"

# WHY CREE
# IS THE FUNNIEST OF
# ALL LANGUAGES

{ TOMSON HIGHWAY }

F THE three to six thousand languages linguists have determined exist in the world—the prevalence of dialects makes it impossible to pin down a number—each has its own special genius. I am fortunate enough to be familiar with three of these: English, French and the language I spoke to the exclusion of all others until age seven, Cree.

English is an intellectual, cerebral language. It comes from, and lives in, the head, and does so in a manner most brilliant. French, *par contre,* is an emotional language, a language of the senses. It comes from, and lives in, the heart. *And* in the stomach. If you don't believe me, try calling your loved one "my cabbage, my lamb, my rabbit, my duck, my pussy, my pet, my casserole dish" with a straight face and see what kind of reaction you get. In French, it makes perfect sense to talk this sensually; in English, it is downright embarrassing. If you still don't believe me, try travelling back and forth between France and

England and see what kind of food you find in each country. In one, the food is fantastic, utterly divine. If, as legend has it, the Inuit have forty words for snow, then the French have easily 350 words for cheese, some of which "orgasm" their way down your throat, which is the only way I have ever been able to describe the sensation in English. *Foie gras?* You die of the senses when you eat it and then float up to heaven. And then there is the wine. In England, by comparison, the food is decidedly *un*-fantastic, shall we say (that's putting it politely). But British Airways? Ho-la-la. The world's best, most efficient, most powerful airline, bar none. Works like a well-oiled engine. Two thousand planes, most of them the size of mansions, that reach all four corners of the world.

Cree, my mother tongue, is neither a language of the mind nor a language of the senses. It is a language of the flesh. A physical language. It lives in the human body not above the neck, as English does, not between the neck and the waist, as French does, but one step lower: between the waist and the thighs. Cree lives in the groin, in the sex organs. It lives, that is to say, in the most fun-loving, the most pleasurable—not to mention the funniest-looking—part of the human corpus: a region of the body that has, for reasons I will posit later, become so alienated from the head that speaking of it in English is a shameful, dirty, embarrassing, disgusting, dare one say evil thing to do.

Since I am writing this essay in English, the part of you that is most alive as you read is your brain. If I were writing in French, and you were reading it accordingly, the most alive parts of you would be your heart and your stomach. Try something as simple as this: *"Bonjour, Barbara, ça va?" "Oui, ça va. Et toi?" "Pas pire. Mais écoute, ma belle, je voudrais te dire quelque chose..."* You see? Your mouth even starts to water when your tongue and lips wrap themselves around those syllables! But if I were writing this in Cree, and you were reading it that way, then what you would be doing is laughing, laughing constantly, laughing so hard your sides would hurt. Somewhere deep inside of you, there would be a zany sensation perpetually on the simmer, perpetually on the verge of exploding into a wild cry of intoxicating, silly, giddy pleasure.

For instance, pronouncing the words syllable by syllable, and at the speed of lightning, say the following: "Winnipeg, Manitoba, Saskatoon, Saskatchewan, Mistassini, Chicoutimi, Chibougamou, Quebec, Temagami, Mattawa, Ottawa, Canada." That, in essence, is Cree. That is the natural rhythm and musicality of the language. Now, with the same feeling, rhythm and speed, say this: *"Neeeeeeeeeeeeeeeeeeeeeeeeeeeeeeeeeeeeeeeeeeeee, awinuk awa oota kaa-pee-pee-tig-weet?"** Practise it until you get it note perfect. You will find, very quickly, that even if you don't have a clue what you are saying, you are already smiling. If you practise it with friends, you will all be laughing. And laughing not lightly, but from the pit of your respective groins. The syllables sound comical not only in and of themselves but in the way they are strung together. It is as if a clown lives inside them. And a clown *does*, in fact, live inside those syllables, of which more in a minute.

Thus far, you know the syllables to the above Cree sentence only with your tongue, your teeth, your lips, your palate and your windpipe. Now on to the meaning. Let's start with the syllable *neee*. As with so many cultural concepts, the word is untranslatable, but we could come close with English expressions such as "oh dear" or "oh my goodness" or "good grief" or "yeah, right" or "you little slut" (in the affectionate, teasing sense) or "you little bastard" (ditto). Then again, *neee* could mean something as simple as "hey." It could even be a combination of the above. You can,

---

* A note on pronunciation: The soft *g*—as in "George" or "gel"—does not exist in the Cree language. All *g*'s are hard, as in "girl" or "gig."

moreover, extend the sound for as long as you want to, depending on how you feel at any given moment, or how silly you want to act, or how you want to stress what you are about to say next. So this *neee*, realistically speaking, could be as short as *neee*. Or it could go on for as long as this (try it): Neeeeeeeeeeeeeeeeeeeee eeeeeeeeeeeeeeeeeeeeeeeeeeeeeeeeeeeeeeeeeeeeeeeeeeeeeeeeeeeeee eeeeeeeeeeeeeeeeeeeeeeeeeeeeeeeeeeeeeeeeeeeeeeeeeeeeeeeeeeeeee eeeeeeeeeeeeeeeeeeeeeeeeeeeeeeeeeeeeeeeeeeeeeeeeeeeeeeeeeeeeee eeeeeeeeeeeeeeeeeeeeeeeeeeeeeeeeeeeeeeeeeeeeeeeeeeeeeeeeeeeeee eeeeeeeeeeeeeeeeeeeeeeeeeeeeeeeeeeeeeeeeeeeeeeeeeeeeeeeeeeeeee eeeeeeeeeeeeeeeeeeeeeeeeeeee. (Hope you remembered to take a great big breath beforehand!) There, I bet you ten dollars you're laughing again. Or at least smiling.

Now try the following at lightning speed: *Chipoo-cheech* (puppy). *Eemana-pitee-pitat* (he's pulling his tooth out). *Eemoomineet* (she's picking berries). *Neeeeeee, aspin eena-mateet* (oops, she's gone, disappeared, *pffft!*). Each syllable, each word is like a tickle in the *kipoo-chim* (blowhole, i.e., rectum); you sit there secretly squirming with visceral pleasure at the same moment as your intellect is being scandalized, especially by the *kipoo-chim*—yikes! Try this on a friend or, better yet, your boss: "Get him in the *kipoo-chim*, bang him in the box." *That* is the Cree sense of humour—utterly ridiculous. It comes shooting out of the language natural as air.

Let's go back to our original sentence and translate it word for word into English. "*Neeeeeeeeeeeeeeeeeeeeeeeeeeeeeeeeeeeeeeeeeeeee, awinuk awa oota kaa-pee-pee-tig-weet?*" *Neee* we've discussed already. Next is *awinuk*, which means "who" (as it does in Ojibway, Blackfoot, Mi'kmaq, and at least thirty other Algonquian languages). The term *awa*, roughly speaking, turns the *awinuk* into a question, as in "who is this?" or "who is that?" *Oota* means "here." *Pee-tig-weet* means, roughly, "coming in"; in this case, by its context, "coming in the door," even though the door itself (*isk-wa-teem*) is not specified. (*"Pee-tig-weet!"* means "Come in!"—the greeting you call when someone comes knocking at your door.) And the *kaa-pee* in front of the *pee-tig-weet* turns the "coming in" into an immediate event, as in "coming in the door just now, right at this moment." So there you go. What the sentence means in its entirety, in English, is: "Hey, who is coming in the door?"

Now I ask you: Is that sentence funny in English? As a fluent English-speaker, permit me to answer the question for you: it is *not* funny, not in the least. Nothing inside you laughs for even a fraction of a second. But in Cree, the sentence is not only funny, it is hysterical; one might even say there is a cartoonish quality to it. It is as if Porky Pig or Bugs Bunny or Elmer Fudd is about to enter through that door. And that is the visceral reality of the Cree language.

As I roam the world physically and intellectually and slide ever so gracefully into my fifties, I find myself unravelling year by year the meaning of one truly fascinating piece of information. And that piece of information is this: When Christopher Columbus arrived in North America in October of the year 1492—a date arguably among the most important in our history as a people—probably the most significant item of baggage he had on his ship was the extraordinary story of a woman who talked to a snake in a garden and, in so doing, precipitated the eviction of humankind from that garden. This seminal narrative has created severe trauma in the lives of many, many people and ultimately, one might argue, the life of our entire planet. I don't think it is any coincidence that the mythology/theology this story comes from, Christianity, has at its centre the existence of a solo god who is male and male entirely.

Such a narrative—the eviction from a garden—most explicitly does *not* exist in Native North American mythology/ theology (which also has not a monotheistic but a pantheistic super-structure or dream world). The Sinai Peninsula, at least as it appeared in Columbus's monotheistic world view, may have been a parched, treeless desert cursed by a very angry male god, but North America, our home and Native land, certainly was not. Quite the contrary: our land is blessed with the most extraordinary, lake-filled, forest-rich, food-filled, mind-boggling beauty. And North America is a landscape blessed most generously, most copiously, by a benevolent female god, one known to us, in the English language, as our Mother, the Earth.*

And then there is our Mother's son/daughter, that insane, hermaphroditic progeny of hers, so endlessly shape-shifting and malleable that *he,* if need be, can turn *her*self, amoeba-like, into any number of different characters. I speak here, of course, of the Trickster, that cosmic clown, that laughing deity whose duty is to teach us a fundamental lesson: that the reason for our existence on this planet is not to suffer, not to wallow in guilt, but to celebrate the experience of living, to eat from the Tree of Knowledge as often, and with as much gusto, as we can.

If languages, as I have come to believe, are shaped by mythologies, world views, collective dream worlds, then English is indelibly marked by that first eviction from the garden. And to this day, the language stops at the gate to that garden. It is forbidden, by an angel who guards the gate jealously with a large flaming sword, to *ever* re-enter. English speakers are *not* to partake of the Tree of Knowledge, laden with the most delicious fruit there is. Only God can do so; such pleasure as is to be found in the garden is reserved exclusively for His enjoyment. Cree, by comparison, did not give birth to a culture of jumbo jets

---

* As is true in all Native North American languages (all that I know of, anyway), Cree has no pronouns that distinguish between "he" and "she" or possessives that make a distinction between "her" and "his." The closest the language comes is a combined form: "he/she" and "her/his." In that sense, regardless of whether we are male biologically or female biologically, we are all "he/she's." As is God, one would think.

that circumnavigate the globe with the efficiency of clockwork. Nor does it have a national literature that has helped to shape world history; not yet, anyway. But try speaking Cree in a virgin forest on some northern lake and you will find, very quickly, that it is pure genius.

In Cree, there is no gate blocking the entrance to—or the exit from—the garden. There is no angel with a flaming sword put there to thwart us. We are allowed into that garden of joy, that garden of beauty, to gambol about as much as we want to. The Trickster—Weesageechak in Cree, Nanabush in Ojibway, Itkomi in Sioux, Raven on the West Coast, Glooscap on the East, Coyote on the Plains—also lives inside the garden. And lives there most pleasurably, sparking to life the syllables of a language that expresses the shudder of excitement that springs from the heart of that garden, from the very Tree of Knowledge itself, a tree that is, as we speak, being tweaked and tickled and pinched and... well... you don't even wanna *know*. In English, you can't. In English, you are not allowed to talk like that. You will go to Hell. (Or, at the very least, you will not get published.) So stop it!

Here, for purposes of comparison, is a creation myth that should knock the socks right off your English-speaking feet and, in the process, make you laugh until you're bent over double. There are many creation myths across Native North America, and many of them are untranslatable into English. Still, let me try this one on you. It comes to us from the Blackfoot Nation of southern Alberta/northern Montana. The Blackfoot are related to us Cree, not least in language, both tongues rising from Algonquian roots as they do. I choose this story because I think it illustrates, to perfection, the humour at the essence of the Trickster, whose energy spreads into all corners of the Native North American dream world. One small request: Please pretend you are reading this story not in English but in Cree.

. . . . . . . .

IN THE BEGINNING there were only two human beings in this world, Old Man Coyote and Coyote Woman. Old Man Coyote lived on one side of the world, Coyote Woman on the other. By chance, they met.

"How strange," said Old Man Coyote. "We are exactly alike."

"I don't know about that," said Coyote Woman. "You're holding a bag. What's inside it?"

Old Man Coyote reached into his bag and brought out a penis. "This odd thing."

"It is indeed an odd thing," said Coyote Woman. "It looks funny. What is it for?"

"I don't know," said Old Man Coyote. "I don't know what to use it for. What do you have inside your bag?"

Coyote Woman dug deep into her bag and came up with a vagina. "You see," she said, "we are not alike. We carry different things inside our bags. Where should we put them?"

"I think we should put them into our navels," said Old Man Coyote. "The navel seems to be a good place for them."

"No, I think not," said Coyote Woman. "I think we should stick them between our legs. Then they will be out of the way."

"Well, all right," said Old Man Coyote. "Let's put them there." So they placed these things between their legs.

"You know," said Coyote Woman, "it seems to me that the strange thing you have there would fit this odd thing of mine."

"Well, you might be right," said Old Man Coyote. "Let's find out." So Old Man Coyote stuck his penis into Coyote Woman's vagina.

"Umm, that feels good," said Coyote Woman.

"You are right," said Old Man Coyote. "It feels very good indeed. I have never felt this way before."

"Neither have I," said Coyote Woman. "It's occurred to me that this might be the way to make other human beings. It would be nice to have company."

"It certainly would," said Old Man Coyote. "Just you and me could become boring."

"Well, in case doing what we just did should result in bringing forth more human beings, what should they look like?" said Coyote Woman.

"Well, I think they should have eyes and a mouth going up and down."

"No, no," said Coyote Woman. "Then they would not be able to see well, and food would dribble out of the lower corner of their mouths. Let's have their eyes and mouths go crosswise."

"I think that the men should order the women about," said Old Man Coyote, "and that the women should obey them."

"We'll see about that," said Coyote Woman. "I think that the men should pretend to be in charge and that the women should pretend to obey, but that in reality, it should be the other way around."

"I can't agree to this," said Old Man Coyote.

"Why quarrel?" said Coyote Woman. "Let's just wait and see how it will work out."

"All right, let's wait and see. How should the men live?"

"The men should hunt, kill buffalo and bears, and bring the meat to the women. They should protect the women at all times," said Coyote Woman.

"Well, that could be dangerous for the men," said Old Man Coyote. "A buffalo bull or a bear could kill a man. Is it fair to put the men in such danger? What should the women do in return?"

"Why, let the women do the work," said Coyote Woman. "Let them cook, and fetch water, and scrape and tan hides with buffalo brains. Let them do all these things while the men take a rest from hunting."

"Well, then, we agree upon everything," said Old Man Coyote. "Then it's settled."

"Yes," said Coyote Woman. "And now why don't you stick that funny thing of yours between my legs again?"

· · · · · · · ·

SO THERE YOU GO. In one group's collective world view, the act of creation is inseparable from an act of rage: revenge on humankind for engaging in physical pleasure, the eating of fruit from a certain tree. In the other, the act of creation is an act of joy, a kick in the pants, one good fuck. In the language of the God—the language of the head—such a human act is gross and unnatural, the apogee of evil. In the language of the goddess— the language of the groin, the womb—it is the most natural act imaginable. When creating the universe and everything in it, one god may have said, "Let there be light," but the other—his wife, the one we never hear of, the one He tried beating to her death with a big sledgehammer—begged to differ. What she said instead was, "Let there be laughter."

# PERFORMING NATIVE HUMOUR

...........................

*The* DEAD DOG *Café*
*Comedy* HOUR

..........

{ THOMAS KING }

*Music to start the show.*

TOM: From Blossom, Alberta, it's The Dead Dog Café Comedy
Hour, with your host, Jasper Friendly Bear...

JASPER: That was a little flat, Tom. Could you try to sound a little more enthusiastic?

GRACIE: And funny. Nobody likes a grouch.

TOM: Okay... From Blossom, Alberta, it's The Dead Dog Café
Comedy...

GRACIE: We didn't say silly.

JASPER: Gracie's right, Tom. Making people laugh and making
a fool of yourself aren't the same.

In the last five years or so, Native humour has become a minor
subject of discussion—not so much on reserves or in urban

centres, mind you, but within the academy, where the creation and explication of such subjects is encouraged and where it can lead to publications and promotions. And in this regard, two things have happened. One, we've decided that Native humour exists, and, two, we've come up with a general definition. Or description. Or good guess.

We say of Native humour that it's about survival, that the only way Native people have been able to endure the array of oppressions that have been visited on us is through humour. And we say that Native humour is about community, that the humour itself does not exclude, that it is not the kind of ad hominem humour you hear on late-night talk shows, for example, where individuals are targeted and the audience is encouraged to laugh at them, at their expense.

Certainly if you looked at the plays of Tomson Highway and Drew Hayden Taylor, or the novels of Eden Robinson and Robert Alexie, where the community creates the humour and participates in it, you might be tempted to go with the communal definition. But to say that humour is about survival is not to mark it as Native, and to say that humour is communal is simply to state the obvious. It's not that these ideas are right or wrong; they simply won't stand as a definition for anything. Black humour, for example, if there is such a thing, could well be about survival, and it may well be communal.

The Native writer and critic W.S. Penn, in his book *Feathering Custer*, talks about satire and burlesque, and suggests that, in terms of humour, we need to encourage satire because, while burlesque is often funny, it "usually laughs at someone's foibles or curious habits" and runs the risk of being cruel, even savage. Satire, on the other hand, "pokes fun at something in such a way that we recognize our connection to it, see in an instant of self-awareness that 'somethingness' in ourselves; and in laughing as a group, we are laughing at ourselves and a community of selves in a way that can even evoke change or induce understanding of the satirized behavior." Penn doesn't suggest that satire is at the heart of Native humour, or that Native humour is satire, but the idea of a community of selves laughing as a group at ourselves is a tempting idea.

So let's get something straight from the beginning. While I'm certainly a member in good standing in the academy, I'm not sure that a valid definition of Native humour exists. If I were threatened with bodily harm, I would probably find myself saying that Native humour is humour that makes Native people laugh, and hope that you didn't ask me to define a Native.

Frankly, I'd have an easier time keeping my footing in the surf at high tide.

I suspect that we will never find a good definition for Native humour, that the definition may lie in and change with performance, which is a fancy way of saying that, if there is such a thing as Native humour, it's like the wind. We can't see it. We don't know where it comes from. And the only time we feel it is when it's blowing in our face.

JASPER: Well, Gracie, what delectable delicacy do you have for our listeners today?
GRACIE: Delectable delicacy?
JASPER: What's to eat?
GRACIE: Oh. Well, today, I thought I'd make one of my favourite recipes... Puppy Stew!
JASPER: Oh, boy! That's one of my favourites. It's one of Tom's, too.
TOM: Actually, I've never had... Puppy Stew?
GRACIE *(slightly disgusted)*: Urban Indians. *(pause)* Here, give me a hand with this box.
*Sound of someone lifting a box and putting it on a table. Sound of puppy whimpering. Sound of a puppy struggling in a box.*

TOM: Gracie...there's something in the box.

GRACIE: I should certainly hope so.

TOM: Something...alive?

*Sound of box being opened.*

JASPER: Hey, Tom, look at this.

*Sound of puppy whimpering.*

TOM: It's a...puppy.

*Sound of happy puppy.*

GRACIE: Hand me that big knife.

When I created *The Dead Dog Café,* I did not set out to create a show that would showcase Native humour. I just wanted to do a radio show that was funny. But because I'm Native and because Floyd Favel Starr and Edna Rain are Native and because we used Native language, Native situations, other Native personalities and as many bad Native puns as we could find, the natural and appropriate conclusion was that here, at long last, was Native humour. In the flesh. As it were.

JASPER: This one?

TOM: Ah...Gracie...

GRACIE: Yes?

TOM: Gracie...you're not going to butcher that puppy, are you?

GRACIE: Something wrong with that?

TOM: Well...I think it might be against the law to...you know... butcher a puppy on a radio show.

GRACIE: Nobody's going to see.

*Sound of puppy whimpering anxiously.*

JASPER: How's Gracie going to make Puppy Stew if she doesn't...

TOM *(quickly)*: Well, she could just tell our listeners how to make...Puppy Stew.

JASPER: What about lunch?

*The Dead Dog Café* began production in 1997, or maybe it was 1998, though it could have been 1996. Not that it matters. It was CBC's fault, or maybe I should blame Kathleen Flaherty, whom you don't know, or I could blame myself, though I prefer to think of myself as blameless in all things, unless there are witnesses and a video tape.

Let's say it was 1997. Someone will look it up and write to tell me that I've made a mistake, but what the hell. Live dangerously.

I was minding my own business—really, I was—when that woman whom you don't know called and told me that CBC (radio, not television) was looking for new material and did I have any.

I didn't. But that's not enough to stop anyone. And here we have to back up for a moment. I was born in 1943. If you do the math, you'll see that I'm old. Not old old. Not ancient. Just well past anything that could be considered prime. Worse, when I was growing up, we didn't have television. Hard to believe, I know. As a matter of fact, the only person in the neighbourhood who had television was my aunt. Angie was a modern woman, and one of her favourite sayings was "When in Rome, do as the Romans do."

My mother had a small beauty parlour at the end of our house that had once been our carport. It wasn't much, and she didn't make much, and because my father had taken off for parts unknown, she had to do all this on her own. And sometimes when my mother had to work late or go somewhere, my brother and I would go to our aunt's house. Which was okay. Angie had two boys, and, when we were growing up, her oldest son, Howard, was not only my cousin, he was my best friend. So, during those evenings when we stayed at Angie's house, Howard and I would head into the room he shared with his brother and play with his slide projector and listen to the radio.

I loved radio. There's magic in a good program, and in those days there were plenty of them: *The Green Hornet, The Lone Ranger, The Cisco Kid, Inner Sanctum, Jack Benny, Batman,*

*Superman.* We would lie in the dark and let our imaginations run wild. After all, that's what radio was about. Imagination.

Then Angie got a television set. I watched a few of the shows, out of curiosity, and they were awful. So, I went back to radio. But Angie wouldn't hear of it.

"When in Rome," she said, "do as the Romans do."

And after that, whenever my brother and I went to stay with our cousins, we would have to endure television.

*Sound of puppy whimpering.*
TOM: Jasper!
GRACIE: You eat hamburger?
*Sound of a cow.*
TOM: Sure…but…
GRACIE: Pork?
*Sound of a pig.*
TOM: A little…
GRACIE: How about lamb?
*Sound of a lamb.*
GRACIE: Any of this sinking in?
JASPER: And while Tom and Gracie are working out Gracie's recipe for Puppy Stew, it's time for Friendly Bear's Blackout Bingo.

You probably think I'm an old crank. But the fact of the matter is you lose a lot with television. It didn't engage my imagination as radio did, and it still doesn't. Part of the problem is that television tends to be formulaic and prescriptive when it doesn't have to be, and because it is both oral and visual and boxed in by time and commercials, it limits some of the imaginative interplay that radio allows.

Though to be fair, radio is oral and boxed in by time and commercials, as well.

Okay, so I don't have a good argument. I still like radio better than television, and when Kathleen Flaherty called me and asked if I had anything for radio, I got to thinking that what I'd like to do was to create an old-time radio show, the kind of thing I listened to when I was a kid.

*Sound of bingo balls rattling around in a cage.*

JASPER: Here's how it works. First you make up your own card. Then each program, we'll call a number. When you get your card blacked out, just write us at Box 555, Edmonton, Alberta, T5J 2P4, and we'll send you a nifty prize.

*Sound of bingo balls.*

JASPER: All right...the first number is...

TOM: Wait a minute...make up your own card?

JASPER: Well, you can make up more than one if you have the time.

TOM: No, no. That's not what I mean.

GRACIE: Tom's worried about people cheating.

JASPER: Why would they do that?

GRACIE (*scornfully*): Urban Indians.

JASPER: Tom, the prizes aren't that good.

Now, in our discussion of Native humour, some of you are probably wondering what exactly Native people have to be happy about. Good question. Actually, not very much. Poverty, unemployment, drugs, disease, depression, governmental paternalism, sports mascots, Hollywood stereotypes, just to name the usual suspects. So it's a good thing that humour is not necessarily about happiness, any more than it is about laughter.

By the way, did you know that when the United States was bombing the hell out of the Marshall Islands (in the good old nuclear-testing days), they named some of their bombs after Indian tribes?

TOM: Look, forget I mentioned it. Okay?

JASPER: Here, why don't you call the first number.

TOM: I'd rather not.

GRACIE: Read the number!

*Bingo balls rattle. Sound of one ball dropping.*

TOM: Ah... B-8.

JASPER: So, Tom, do you have B-8 on your bingo card?

TOM: Jasper, I don't have a bingo card.

GRACIE: So, what are you waiting for?

JASPER: Okay, Tom, that takes care of bingo. What's next?

When I was a young man, I moved to Salt Lake City. Mormon country, home to one of the few homegrown North American religions. Brigham Young. Joseph Smith. Polygamy. A remarkably businesslike religion. A natural extension of covenant theology. Humans and God agreeing that success in business is an economic indicator of spiritual grace. And salvation.

It was a job that got me there. The Counselor to Native Students. That was me. At first I had a hard time separating the people from the religion, for Mormon theology has a decidedly racist angle to it. Black people were the Sons of Ham and cursed. Indians, Mexicans and South Pacific Islanders were Lamanites, who would, in the fullness of time, turn "white and delightsome."

I always liked that phrase. "White and delightsome." As if it were a reward. As if it were something to look forward to.

Some of that changed when the then head of the church, Spencer W. Kimball, had a revelation concerning blacks. God, it seemed, had changed his mind, and the Mormon faithful could welcome the Sons of Ham into the fold. The progressive element of the church rejoiced at this good news, in much the same way that stockbrokers welcome a bull market. The conservative element threatened to secede, though in the end that was more noise than substance. And predictably, with the burden of segregation lifted, the church expanded its proselytizing activities into Africa.

The cynic in me knew that the religion wasn't the individual. Some of my best friends were Mormon. But I also knew that neither were a few enlightened parishioners the measure of the religion.

So we had a good time with the church, made jokes at its expense, laughed at the revelation as both an opportunist moment to open new markets and an attempt to try to gloss over the inherent racism of orthodox church doctrine.

It was Flannery O'Connor, I think, who said that there's no pleasure but meanness. She wasn't thinking about me, I'm sure, but she could have been.

*Sound of a puppy whimpering.*
JASPER: Oh, right. You guys get that recipe worked out yet?
GRACIE: You won't believe what he did.
JASPER: The puppy?
*Sound of puppy.*
GRACIE: No. What's-his-name.
JASPER: Tom? What did Tom do?
GRACIE: He named the puppy.

At about the same time we were having all this fun with Mormon theology, we were also organizing Indian Awareness Days, a once-a-year event that was supposed to help raise awareness of Native people and the problems we faced. As the Counselor to Native Students, it was my job to invite speakers to come to Salt Lake and speak with the kinds of audiences that you get on a university campus.

That particular year, we invited a Hopi elder, a man named Thomas Bianca, to give the keynote address. We took him out to dinner ahead of time (a Native bonding ritual) and we told him all about the church and the revelation. And then we told him our best jokes. He smiled at most of them and, when we had finished with our clever stories, when we had run out of wit and wisdom, he said that it was too bad there weren't more people who could laugh at them.

I was too young and too dumb then to understand what Bianca had just told me. But I remembered it, partly because there was something about the way he said it that gave it a sense of importance.

JASPER: He didn't.
GRACIE: Cuddles.
JASPER: Tom, you named lunch Cuddles?
TOM: I had a dog named Cuddles. When I was a kid.
GRACIE: Well, now you have another. Here.
*Sound of puppy and the box.*
TOM: I don't want a puppy.
GRACIE: Tough.
TOM: Hey, I got an idea.

A few years after my stint in Utah, I moved to northern California and took a job as Associate Dean for Student Affairs at Humboldt State University. I was in charge of a number of what were then called "ethnic programs": Upward Bound, the Education Opportunity Program and Special Services. They were actually low-income programs, and while they did bring African-Americans, Mexican-Americans, Native-Americans and other hyphenated folks to that campus on the northern coast of California, they brought in White-Americans as well.

Every so often we would have a get-together, a luncheon or a barbecue, some kind of social, to try to create a sense of community among the students in all the programs. At these events, the conversation would always turn to matters of race and racism. I didn't think much about it, probably even joined in myself. Until one of the students came by my office to tell me that she was dropping out.

There were a great many reasons why students in these programs quit. Many found the academics simply too hard. Others had families they had to help financially. A few found the university environment cold and hostile. But the student who sat across my desk from me was a good student who had done very well her first year, a student whose family was thrilled that she was at university. So, I thought it was the environment problem.

But it wasn't.

GRACIE: This I want to hear.

TOM: No, really. Here's what we do. *(beat)* We have a contest.

GRACIE: Forget the contest. I'll just take Cuddles into the kitchen and wring its little...

TOM *(quickly)*: NO! *(beat)* Look, we'll use Cuddles as the prize in the contest.

JASPER: I don't know, Tom. I'm pretty hungry. What about you, Gracie?

GRACIE: Starving.

That student I was telling you about wanted to leave university because she didn't feel comfortable in the programs and was depressed much of the time. Every time there's a get-together, she told me, everyone complains about whites and racism. All the jokes are about whites and how they've treated ethnic people badly and how whites don't have a culture. It's okay if you're black, she said, or Native, but I'm white.

I tried to tell her that no one meant her, but it didn't do any good, and I'm not sure that I believed my own assurances. Thomas Bianca had been right. Community depends on everyone sharing in the stories that the community tells. All those years ago, when Bianca had told me that it was too bad there weren't more people to laugh at our jokes, he was gently reminding me that humour is only truly funny when it is inclusive, that humour that excludes is, in the end, a weapon.

TOM: Wait! Wait! It'll be good publicity for the show.
JASPER: We don't need publicity, Tom. CBC is public radio.
TOM: Well, you can't butcher a puppy on public radio!
JASPER: *(sigh)* What else do we have for lunch?
GRACIE: Macaroni.
TOM: I love macaroni!

I sing with a drum group. The Way-Chee-Wasa Singers. *Way-chee-wasa* is an Ojibway word that means (if I've got it right) "far away." Sandy Benson, who is Ojibway, gave us this name because everyone (except Sandy and Mike) came from someplace else. Harold Rice is a Salish carver. John Samosi is a Métis craftsman from Saskatchewan, Mike Duke is Ojibway and an RCMP officer. I'm Cherokee, as is my son, Benjamin. Oh, and Sandy is a visual artist and drives a school bus. Culturally, we have nothing in common, but when we get together, which is all too seldom these days, we spend a good deal of time making jokes about our failings and laughing at ourselves.

Is that Native humour? Self-reflexive satire? Of course we could forgo trying to define Native humour and look at the kind of humour to which Native people are drawn.

*Puppy grunting sounds.*
GRACIE: Oh, great. Look what your dog just did on my clean floor.
TOM: It's not my dog!
JASPER: Holy! Look at that. And such a little puppy.
GRACIE: The shovel's out back.
TOM: I'm not getting near that.

*Music to end the show.*

JASPER: Well, that's all the time we have this week.

GRACIE: Don't forget the bucket.

JASPER: From the Dead Dog Café in Blossom, Alberta, this is Jasper Friendly Bear...

GRACIE: And Gracie Heavy Hand...

TOM: And Tom King...

*Sound of puppy.*

TOM: ...and Cuddles, saying...

ALL: So long for now!

JASPER: And don't forget...Stay calm.

GRACIE: Be brave.

JASPER: Wait for the signs.

There are probably cultural differences in humour, but I suspect what makes Native people laugh is pretty much what makes all people laugh. Sure we laugh at misfortunes and we laugh at catastrophes and we laugh at sexist and racist jokes, but these moments do not define our humour so much as they define our fears and our hatreds. We are at our best when we laugh at ourselves.

*Music ends.*

JASPER: You know, we're getting a lot better with this radio show thing.

TOM: No, we're not.

GRACIE: Next time I'm cooking moose stew. Let's see what Tom does with that.

*Sound of a trumpeting elephant.*

TOM: Wait a minute. That wasn't a moose.

When *The Dead Dog Café* was still in its heyday, I got a letter from a listener who wanted to know why Jasper and Gracie

always picked on Tom and why he always came out on the short
end of the stick. It was a nice letter, but the inference was that
Native people were supposed to treat each other better. I wrote
back and said the fact that Jasper and Gracie included Tom in
their story was proof that they liked him, that he was a part of
their community, and the reason that Tom always came out on
the short end of the stick was simply because it was his place in
the story.

GRACIE: Lucky guess.
JASPER: Not to worry, Tom. Hardly anyone in Canada knows
　　what a moose sounds like.
TOM: I knew.
JASPER: *Au contraire,* Tom.

My family and I went to France one summer and toured the
Loire Valley. My partner, Helen, is fond of guidebooks and had
brought one along for the occasion. And as we toured the grand
châteaux that run the length of the valley like fast-food fran-
chises, Helen would read the guidebook, telling us what we were
looking at. At one point, she spent so much time with her head
in the book, reading about the beauty of the château ceilings
above her, that she never saw them and we had to go back and
walk the corridors again.

GRACIE: That's French for on the contrary.
TOM: I know what it means.
JASPER: Knowing what an elephant sounds like is not necessar-
　　ily the same thing as knowing what a moose sounds like.
GRACIE: Elephants are easy. *(beat)* What about this?
*Sound of a cat.*
TOM: That's a cat.
*Sound of a bird.*

TOM: That's a bird.

GRACIE: Sure, but what kind?

TOM: I don't know…a crow?

JASPER: No, Tom, it's a Moosebird.

GRACIE: See?

TOM: There is no such thing as a Moosebird!

JASPER: *Au contraire,* Tom.

Maybe, like in the guidebook story, we don't need a definition of something we can see and hear, if we simply pay attention. Besides, what would we do with a definition of Native humour anyway? We'd just waste time trying to apply the definition, and we might miss the performance. Worse, we might try to insist that Native humour measure up to the definition, even though we know that humour will change while definitions, once struck, will not.

GRACIE: That's French for…

TOM *(annoyed)*: I know what it means!

JASPER: So, Tom, what do you and Cuddles have planned for the rest of the day?

*Sound of a happy Cuddles.*

TOM: Jasper…

JASPER: Yes, Tom?

TOM: Jasper…

*Ad lib to end.*

Besides, trying to define Native humour, in any formal way, would require close readings, footnotes and several panel discussions. In the end, it's probably wiser and more judicious to put nothing in writing and pretend we know what we're talking about, so that, when the need arises, we can change our minds and never have to worry about being wrong. Or right.

*Astutely* selected **ETHNO-BASED**
examples of **CULTURAL** *jocularity* and
*racial* **COMICALNESS**

. . . . . . . .

{ **EXAMPLE 18** }

*"Why did the chicken cross the road?"*

COLONIZED INDIAN: *"Chickens should never cross a road that white men have built before the Great White Father crosses it first. If the White Father crosses it, it is good. We must then follow."*

GRASSROOTS INDIAN: *"If the darn chickens need to get across the road, let 'em cross the darn road!"*

NEW AGE INDIAN: *The chicken decided to cross the road after Freudian dream therapy, drumming, sweat lodges, time with my shaman and long walks on the beach near my beach house.*

INAC INDIAN: *"Chickens cross the road because CFR 49, Section 11299, gives them the authority to do so. They wrote a grant proposal and we funded them. We are very proud of them."*

POWWOW INDIAN: *"That chicken must have been heading to a forty-nine!"*

{ **EXAMPLE 19** }

TWO NATIVE WOMEN *who had just met were having tea one day. One woman was absolutely amazed to find out the other woman had ten children all named Lloyd.*

"Why did you call all your children Lloyd?" the woman asked her new friend.

"It's a great time saver. I can just yell 'Lloyd, time for bed' or 'Lloyd, dinner time,' and they all will come. This way I don't have to repeat myself."

The other woman wasn't convinced. "But don't you find it a little confusing? What if you only wanted or needed one specific child? Say... the second youngest or the oldest? How do you get their attention?"

"Oh that's easy," said the mother. "Then I just call them by their last name."

{ EXAMPLE 20 }

DURING THE FRENCH AND INDIAN WAR, the Mohawk Nation was allied with the British. One day a French regiment was marching towards an important fort when the scouts spotted a lone Mohawk warrior standing on top of a hill.

The regimental commander issued an order to have a squad of men apprehend the warrior for questioning. The commander then watched through his spyglass as the squad approached the Mohawk. The warrior waited until the last moment before stepping forward and grabbing the nearest French soldier by the throat. The scuffle kicked up so much dust that the commander couldn't see what was going on. After a few minutes, the dust settled to reveal the Mohawk warrior still standing, with the bodies of the French soldiers strewn on the ground around him.

Outraged, the commander ordered a full platoon up the hill to capture the Mohawk. But the result was the same. Next, an entire company was sent up the hill. This time, the Mohawk took his war club in hand. After several minutes, when the dust cleared, the commander was again astounded to see the Mohawk *standing amidst the scores of bodies of French soldiers. One bruised and bloody soldier could be seen staggering back down the hill. The survivor was quickly led to the commander to report on what had happened.*

*"Don't send any more men up the hill, sir. It's a trap!" groaned the wounded man. "He's got a Mohawk woman up there with him!"*

{ EXAMPLE 21 }

THESE TWO INDIANS *walk out of a bar...*
    *Hey, it could happen.*

# ABOUT THE
# CONTRIBUTORS

． ． ． ． ． ． ． ． ． ． ． ． ． ．

A contemporary Koko (Koochum), JANICE ACOOSE balances her
time among family, work and weight training. Her two *Noo'sims*—
Alijah and Angelina—have taught her how to laugh and play,
activities that balance the professorial duties she performs at
the First Nations University of Canada. Unlike most professors,
Acoose is more inclined to be heard bragging up her fifty-year-
old weight-trained body than her body of published work.

NATASHA BEEDS is a sessional lecturer in the Department of
English at the First Nations University of Canada's Saskatoon
campus. She has a blend of Cree and Caribbean ancestry and is
an avid martial artist with a black belt in Tae Kwon Do. These
three diverse influences combine to give her a unique perspective with which to approach life. Currently, she is in the process
of returning to university to pursue a master's degree in English
and Indigenous Studies with a focus on indigenous literatures.

KRISTINA FAGAN is a member of the Labrador Métis Nation who grew up in St. John's, Newfoundland. She teaches Aboriginal literature in the Department of English at the University of Saskatchewan.

IAN FERGUSON won the 2004 Stephen Leacock Memorial Medal for Humour for his book *Village of the Small Houses: A Memoir of Sorts*. With his brother Will Ferguson, he is the co-author of the bestseller *How to Be a Canadian,* which was shortlisted for the Leacock and won the CBA Libris Award for the best non-fiction book of 2002. He performed the role of Amos in the premiere production of Drew Hayden Taylor's *The Buz'Gem Blues.*

KAREN FROMAN is a green-eyed Mohawk who grew up on the prairies. She recently finished an MA in Native Studies and is currently working towards her PhD. Karen lives in Winnipeg with her two kids, three cats and one hamster.

TOMSON HIGHWAY is the proud son of legendary caribou hunter and world-championship dogsled racer Joe Highway. Born in a tent pitched in a snowbank, he comes from the extreme northwest corner of Manitoba, where the province meets Saskatchewan and Nunavut. Today, he writes plays, novels and music for a living. Among his best-known works are the plays *The Rez Sisters* and *Dry Lips Oughta Move to Kapuskasing* and the bestselling novel *Kiss of the Fur Queen.*

MIRJAM HIRCH, MA, is Fellow for Traditional Healing Arts and Sciences at the Center for World Indigenous Studies in Olympia, Washington. She is a doctoral student in the Department of Geography at the University of Cologne, Germany.

DON KELLY is from the Ojibways of Onigaming First Nation, a Treaty 3 reserve in northwestern Ontario. He's been a stand-up comic since the early 1990s, working at clubs and gatherings across the nation and appearing on such shows as CBC's *Comics!*, CBC Radio's *Madly Off in All Directions* and CTV's *Comedy Now!* He currently lives in Ottawa.

THOMAS KING, an award-winning writer and scholar of Cherokee and Greek descent, is a professor of English at the University of Guelph. His widely acclaimed novels include *Medicine River, Truth & Bright Water* and *Green Grass, Running Water.* King presented the 2003 Massey Lectures. His popular CBC Radio series, *The Dead Dog Café*, is being adapted as an animated television series.

LOUISE PROFEIT-LEBLANC is a storyteller who hails from the Nacho N'yak Dun First Nation in Yukon Territory. She has been practising the art for almost twenty-five years and was privileged to be taught by the best of the storytellers from the North, including Angela Sidney, Tommy McGinty, Kitty Smith, Joe Henry and Kenneth Nukon. A co-founder of the Yukon International Storytelling Festival and the Society of Yukon Artists of Native Ancestry, she served as Native Heritage Advisor for the Yukon government and is presently Aboriginal Arts Coordinator for the Canada Council for the Arts in Ottawa.

ALLAN J. RYAN is a singer/songwriter/satirist and the author of *The Trickster Shift: Humour and Irony in Contemporary Native Art.* He holds the New Sun Chair in Aboriginal Art and Culture at Carleton University in Ottawa.

DREW HAYDEN TAYLOR has done everything from performing stand-up comedy at the Kennedy Center in Washington, D.C., to lecturing on the films of Sherman Alexie at the British Museum in London, England. He is the author of several award-winning plays, fifteen books, numerous television scripts and various documentaries (most notably one on Native humour, *Redskins, Tricksters and Puppy Stew,* which he also directed for the National Film Board of Canada). His Native humour column appears in newspapers across Canada. He is an Ojibway from the Curve Lake First Nation.

# ACKNOWLEDGEMENTS

................................

*A* LOT OF people inspired me to put this book together. I guess it all started with my mother and family back in Curve Lake, who taught me the importance of a good laugh. And I'm still laughing at them today. (Just kidding.)

This book would not have come about without *Redskins, Tricksters and Puppy Stew,* my National Film Board documentary about Native humour. Special thanks to producer Silva Basmajian, Lockwood Productions and everybody else involved with that fabulous project. One of these days I will learn to hit a golf ball properly.

The next people to be thanked are the contributors to this book, who took the time and expended the energy to put down on paper their musings about what makes Native humour so special. I hope I did you proud.

Other people who have figured in the development of this book or supplied ideas or jokes include Dawn Dumont, David Deleary, Darrel Dennis, Herbie Barnes, Phil Belfry, Ken Williams, Tyrone Tootoosis and Kim Ziervogel. Special thanks to Janine Willie.